The Perfect Money Plan

BY JULIE HEDGE

"I hope you realise you're setting my
behaviour patterns so that I get myself
hopelessly into debt in later life."

an
ovolo
book

**Ovolo Books Ltd
Unit 10 Brook Farm,
Ellington, Huntingdon,
Cambridgeshire
PE28 0AE**

This edition © Ovolo Books 2009
Text © Julie Hedge 2009

First published 2009

Design: Gill Lockhart
Cartooms: Cartoonstock

ISBN: 978-1-905959-037

Printed by the MPG Books Group
in the UK

For more great Ovolo titles visit:
www.ovolobooks.co.uk

The Pocket Money Plan

- Give the right pocket money
- Encourage saving and earning
- Teach how to spend wisely
- Instill the budgeting habit
- Show how borrowing works

BY JULIE HEDGE

The Pocket Money Plan

DEDICATION

FOR PAUL

HOW THIS BOOK CAME ABOUT

IF THERE'S ONE thing my husband and I picked up from advising people about money over the years, it was this: every parent wants their child to have a financially secure future. Most of those parents, however, saw their responsibility as saving what they could to give to their child when they were older.

Few of them considered something far more important: teaching money management on a day-to-day basis. Sometimes the reason was a lack of guidance for parents. Often we realised that money matters were a mystery to the adults concerned, never mind the children!

As we were both financial advisers, we tried to persuade investment companies to offer products designed to appeal to children, with money management lessons as an 'add on' to the investment. But we soon discovered that even some of the UK's largest financial institutions weren't interested in teaching kids about money. So I decided to take on the task myself – and the first step was writing this book.

Children today want too much, and sometimes get too much with no thought of how any of it is paid for. I hope this book will help us all to start changing that.

"What is it? It's your first PIN number!"

ABOUT THE AUTHOR

JULIE HEDGE is a native Scot but moved to the South of England when working for a major UK insurance company. For the past 12 years she has headed up her own financial management consultancy. She is frequently quoted in the national press, has appeared on BBC Radio and contributes to various trade magazines giving expert comment.

Julie's husband died suddenly in 2007. She now lives in Surrey with her two young sons and, from time to time, her teenage step daughter.

CONTENTS

"We are giving that kid far too
much pocket money."

The Pocket Money Plan

"The allowance is great dad, but I want
you to know it's not my main motivation
in being your son"

The Pocket Money Plan

USE WHAT YOU'RE ALREADY
SPENDING TO TEACH YOUR CHILD
FINANCIAL HEALTH FOR LIFE

INTRODUCTION

The Pocket Money Plan

For us as parents, the birth of a child is a joyful time. Friends and family come together to celebrate the miracle of a new person joining the human race. Everyone expresses their hope and good wishes for the future. But there's another group of people with a different interest in your child, and they don't show up at the labour ward. To them, your child is a customer.

By the age of two most children can already recognise several well-known commercial logos. By five they are likely to have been exposed to their first half million marketing messages. Before their early teens they will have clear ideas about which food brands they want to eat, which clothes brands they want to wear, which mobile phone is cool. They'll let you know, too. It's not called pester power for nothing.

At the same time, children observe debt all around them – the legacy of a generation of easy credit which has seen regular saving among adults plunge to an all-time low. The modern trend is to have everything now, rather than wait until we can afford it, and for our youngsters the temptation to spend what they don't have is

enormous. One high street store recently ran a marketing campaign that said: 'Want it? Gotta have it!' Their target market? Pre-teen girls. Sadly, this shop is not the only one that should be banished to the naughty step.

On top of that comes the desire to accumulate 'stuff', and keep up appearances. Almost every modern child's bedroom contains a pile of objects which they don't really need, or even want. Just under half of 16 to 24 year-olds (44 per cent) say their friends put pressure on them to keep buying, even when they have run out of money. This mixture of sophisticated marketing, peer pressure and a 'gotta have it' culture is a ferocious cocktail, and few are entirely immune to its effects.

So perhaps it's not surprising that many children are growing up with unrealistic ideas about money. They could almost be forgiven for thinking it comes from winning the lottery, from five minutes of fame on reality TV, from Premiership football – even from the Government. Never mind that lottery wins are a 14 million to one chance, or that for every successful footballer thousands fail.

As a result, personal debt in the UK is increasing at the rate of a million pounds every five minutes. Every four minutes someone is declared insolvent or bankrupt. More than half of England's teenagers owe (or have owed) money by the time they are 17. And the Consumer Credit Counselling Service reports that more and more young people are contacting them for help with debt.

Of course, most young people don't go too badly off track.

The Pocket Money Plan

But the world around them certainly sets a poor example of how to manage money. It's never been more important for children to understand that money is earned, to learn to live within their means, to spend wisely, to resist the marketing hype. These are not options – they are vital life skills. If your child can acquire them early on, he or she will have an advantage as significant as a college or university education.

But how to do it? Bringing up kids to say 'please' and 'thank you' is one thing; instilling financial savvy is something else entirely. One thing's certain: without a specific plan, you're leaving things to chance – or at least unconsciously passing on your own attitudes. That's fine as long one or both of you happens to be a financial whizz. (Sadly, it works the other way too: research shows that parents with serious debt problems tend to transmit that lack of financial awareness to their children.) Most of us fall between those two extremes: we give regular pocket money, which our children spend entirely as they choose; we back that up with the occasional well-intentioned chat; we buy them the bigger things they need; and we hope for the best.

Unfortunately, this approach has two enormous drawbacks. First, lectures are boring. Second, giving children money or things for 'free' fails to teach them how the real world works. As to hoping for the best – well, it's not the ideal tactic to rely on.

But there is a better way to go about it, and that's what this book is about. *The Pocket Money Plan* can enable you to teach your child to manage money for life.

The Pocket Money Plan works because the rules are simple and easy to follow. You do not have to be knowledgeable about money to make it work. In fact, many parents find that using the plan helps build their own financial management skills. And although it has strict rules, you can adapt it to suit your situation and values. It will even help your child discover his or her own values too.

The world may be telling your child: 'Want it? Gotta have it!' The Pocket Money Plan says that spending and saving money well are skills all children need to learn. And they need to be given time to practise them before they become adults.

You can afford to use the Plan whether you're a millionaire, or struggling to make ends meet. And the reason it's so flexible is simple.

You spend the same money you're spending now, in a new way.

A way that provides your child with a financial education.

That in turn means growing up with the confidence to choose the things that are really needed and to do without the stuff that isn't. In today's world, that's a precious gift indeed.

Happiness is not in the mere possession of money; it lies in the joy of achievement, in the thrill of creative effort

FRANKLIN D ROOSEVELT

CHAPTER ONE

THE POCKET MONEY PLAN

The Pocket Money Plan

This chapter outlines the principles of *The Pocket Money Plan*. It explains why you need to stop giving your child things for free, and instead use pocket money as a tool to educate him about money. It looks at how much to give (and when), and what you might expect in return. It also introduces the Give, Spend, Save concept which means that your child can't spend all of the pocket money you give her.

And all of this needn't cost you a penny more than you're spending on him now.

It's a simple plan. It has to be, not only so that your child can understand what's happening but because, if anything is too difficult, we parents just don't have time. There are only six steps, and each one probably holds elements of what you already do. But taken together they offer a new slant on the movement of money between parent and child. And anyone can do it, trust me.

STEP 1
STOP GIVING YOUR CHILD STUFF FOR FREE

There is a huge temptation in all parents to offer our children their every desire on a plate. But giving into that temptation means they will never learn responsible money behaviour. What's worse, as time goes they will cease to appreciate what we give them anyway, and so generosity backfires to create a no-win situation.

Just for a moment, put aside your parent's love and think of yourself as a bank, with your child as the only customer. To date, your child has been the bank's worst nightmare. The funds he or she has required have been enormous, and look set to rise (and rise) for many years. Worse still, the bank has been authorising withdrawals from cash machines where no deposits are required.

This is not how the real world works. So here's the deal: you must stop giving your child stuff for free. The bank needs to get commercial!

What is 'stuff'? It's the things your child doesn't really need, but wants all the same: sweets every time you pass a shop, a DVD when they've got the sniffles, a toy they see on TV. You know what I mean.

For some parents, cutting off the supply of 'stuff' is as hard for them than it is for their shocked offspring. After all, you are

The Pocket Money Plan

weaning not only your child but also yourself off the habit of consuming things for no reason. Some children are so used to hearing 'yes' that they ask without thinking. Encouraged to stop and think, they often realise that they don't really want the 'stuff' in question. This in itself is an important realisation, because it's your child's first step towards managing his or her own money – which includes buying at least some of his or her own 'stuff'.

However, you can't rush straight ahead to that point just yet. If you're going to use *The Pocket Money Plan* to spend the same money you're spending now, in a new way, you first need to know what you actually are spending now! So stage one of *The Pocket Money Plan* begins, as it must, with the grown-up, by asking you to work out how much you are shelling out on 'stuff'.

This can't be a 'finger in the air' approximation. Apart from anything else, any guesstimate you make is likely to be a wild under-estimation. Just as children get used to getting, parents get used to giving. The money you spend may not even register as it quite literally pours from your purse.

I suggest you write down the cost of all 'stuff' for at least two months, and preferably three. That way there will be at least one school holiday in there – which is, let's face it, the time when the bills go sky high.

This day-by-day job of recording details can be tough, especially if you're the kind of person who can't stand lists. Would it help to say that, for many parents, it's the hardest part of implementing

The Pocket Money Plan? Just hang onto the fact that it's the vital first step to lifelong financial health for your child.

Where you write down the amounts you're spending is up to you. But somewhere public like the fridge door should do the trick!

When you have a true picture of what you are spending on 'stuff' (and you've recovered from the shock), you can finally work out how much of your current spend you want to devote to *The Pocket Money Plan*. You may choose to use all of it, or you may go for less (of course, there's nothing to stop you using more, although you'd need a pretty good reason). Whatever amount you settle on, it'll be an informed choice. And you'll have taken the first steps towards controlling not only your child's finances, but also your own.

Banishing free 'stuff' sounds harsh initially. Just remember it cannot possibly harm your child. In fact, as part of *The Pocket Money Plan*, it will do an enormous amount of good. As Step 2 shows...

STEP 2

START GIVING POCKET MONEY INSTEAD

If you stop the free 'stuff', you need to provide an alternative. It will perhaps come as no surprise that the alternative is pocket money.

But not just any old pocket money. You are going to give what may at first seem a surprising amount, in a planned, controlled way.

Just how much to give we'll come to in Step 4. But more important is the way you give it. By being organised (which we'll come to in Step 3), you are giving more than money. You are investing in your child's financial education – and the chances of reward are immense, for both of you.

So how exactly can giving pocket money become an investment? The answer is because it gives your child responsibility.

One of the main characteristics of financially healthy people is the ability to deal with the everyday expenses of living before spending 'the cream at the top'. There's even a term for this kind of behaviour: bottom-up financial planning. Everyday expenses are the non-negotiable bills in life – the ones you cannot avoid if you want to keep a roof over your head. The ability to meet these expenses gives our finances a solid foundation.

Conversely, the reason many people get into debt is because they try to spend the cream at the top before they have paid their everyday expenses. They buy the 'stuff' first (whether it's a holiday, a pair of shoes or whatever) then get into debt because an everyday expense comes along that cannot be avoided. A gas bill, for example. Or maybe the mortgage. This is known as managing your money from the top down, and it is rarely successful.

Unfortunately, bottom-up financial planning is not an inbuilt skill; it is one you have to learn. And *The Pocket Money Plan* is designed to help your child learn it. As children do not get bills (although they create one or two), the Plan creates a couple of 'everyday expenses' which have to be met before the funds for spending are allocated.

Just how we do that comes in the next step...

STEP 3

GIVE, SAVE, SPEND

OK, brace yourself. Not all the money you give your child is meant for spending.

This is the crux of the plan; your child must split the money three ways. Here's how.

GIVE

First of all (and it really is first of all), some of the money you hand over is for your child to give away.

That means a certain proportion will be set aside for charitable causes and acts of kindness. The reasons to encourage this kind of generosity are extremely compelling. Besides creating a socially responsible attitude, it provides your child with an 'everyday expense' which has to be met before spending a single penny on the fun stuff. It's the perfect way to encourage a bottom-up approach to managing money – perhaps the most important kind of money behaviour for children. And there are many other education opportunities besides, which we will return to in Chapter 2.

SAVE

Next, some money should be set aside for saving. Again, this reinforces a bottom-up approach to money. But it also teaches your child a vital life skill – and one all too lacking in today's world. Saving is the only sensible way to deal with sudden, unexpected expenses (the car breaking down), or achieving a long-held dream (such as whale-watching holiday in the Azores).

We are not born with the ability to save, and neither do we instinctively know why saving is so important. So your child needs to be taught how to do it until the habit is formed. It's no different from learning to ride a bike, to be polite, or to eat healthily.

SPEND

Once the Giving and Saving are done, your child can use the remainder for Spending.

Spending seems such an easy art to master. There are so many gadgets, so many marketing ploys, and so many choices that you'd think parting with money is a natural skill. It may well be. But the art of spending wisely is a whole different matter.

As with saving, spending wisely is not an inborn skill – just look at the average level of personal debt. No, spending wisely is a learned behaviour. That's why *The Pocket Money Plan* doesn't just stop after giving and saving. By sticking to cash, at least for the first few years (see Chapter 4), you will enable your child to discover that he or she can only buy *what* they can afford, *when* they can afford it. It's the basis of budgeting – one of the key skills for good money management.

HELPFUL IDEAS
MONEY POTS

To enable your child to grasp the idea of Give, Save, Spend you need a box or jar to put the money in. That way children can always easily divide up their funds. As with any new regime involving kids, try and create some excitement around the whole affair. You might buy some money boxes, or adapt some you already have. Whatever you settle on, the arrangement needs to have three sections. There's an ingeniously designed moneybox at www.pocketmoneyplan. co.uk, created specifically for the Give, Save, Spend concept.

STEP 4
BE CONSISTENT

If by now you're thinking, 'Hey, we do some of this already,' that's good. The Pocket Money Plan is designed to be as familiar as possible. But as with so many things, it's the details which make it all work.

1. DECIDE HOW MUCH POCKET MONEY TO GIVE

This is, of course, going to be different for every family. But the method to work out a fair amount is the same.

First, check if what you're currently spending on 'stuff' is realistic (see Step 1). If it's not, reduce it. This amount, then, is your rule-of-thumb figure for *The Pocket Money Plan* 'spend' fund. The object, after all, is simply to use the amount you spend anyway in a different way; one that provides some financial education.

To date, you've regularly authorised an unlimited, no-strings overdraft to purchase 'stuff'. As this is not how the real world works, you do your children no favours by helping them to think it does. So write down the items you currently provide for free, which you'd now like your child to pay for under *The Pocket*

Money Plan. You can take this as far as you feel is right. If your child is older he or she may end up paying for sweets, haircuts, clothes, toiletries, and so on. If your child's still little, you might provide the basics and expect him or her to pay only for the non-essential items.

What about really big amounts, which might swamp the rest of the calculations? Your child may play an expensive musical instrument, ride a horse, or be a talented sports player, for example. My suggestion in this case is that you ask your child to provide a contribution. It will help teach some responsibility to the rest of the family, and give your child a stake in sticking with it when things get tough. As for hobbies, I promise your child will get fantastic pleasure from using his or her own money to buy something which is cared about – much more so than if you pay.

It might not sound earth-shattering to allow your children to buy for themselves what you would have bought anyway, but it really is different to them. Already they will be learning – and enjoying it, too.

A ROUGH GUIDE

Children vary enormously, but here's a rough baseline to help you arrive at a sensible figure

AGE	GIVE ENOUGH TO BUY*
5-8	sweets
8-10	sweets, hobbies, magazines
10-12	sweets, haircut, hobbies, magazines, music
12-14	sweets, haircut, toiletries, hobbies, clothes, magazines, music
15-18	sweets, haircut, toiletries, hobbies, clothes, magazines, music, school trips, leisure trips

*After deducting money for Giving and Saving

2. AGREE YOUR PERCENTAGES

With your child's spending allowance mapped out, you need to add on the Giving and Saving components.

The percentage for each is up to you and what you can afford. But bear in mind that the disciplines of Giving and Saving are a vital component in teaching your child to manage money. So if you just asked your child to give away 1 per cent, save 4 per cent and go wild with the remaining 95 per cent you might not achieve that much.

If you can afford it, in my view, Giving and Saving should make up at least 30 per cent of the total Pocket Money amount. The formula my children work on is 10 per cent for Giving, 30 per cent for Saving and 60 per cent for Spending. But see how you and your child get on. The amount has to be workable and, above all, affordable. This book promises to show you how to spend what you're already spending in a new way – and whilst that's possible if you can cut out some of the really useless 'stuff', the Giving and Saving elements can also end up costing you extra. If that happens in your case, think of it as the cost of your child's financial education. We parents pay for football lessons, karate lessons, and countless more besides. Think of the Giving and Saving funds as the cost of their money lessons.

3. PAY ON TIME, EVERY TIME

Having decided on the amount, set out dates and times of payment. This is likely to be weekly (for younger children) or monthly (when they are reaching their teens).

It may sound silly, but you need to actually give the money when you say you will. How many of us have promised we'll give pocket money and not actually done it? Not paying is no longer good enough. Decide you are going to do it and stick to it.

Remember, this is business. You are The Bank and *The Pocket Money Plan* is your best-selling product. The contract terms must be adhered to. Your child is your customer. If you don't show your child a model of good behaviour, you can't expect it back.

A written record of your contract terms, signed by both of you, is a good idea. Then there can be no arguments if things go wrong.

4. STICK TO CASH

As important as timing is handing over the loot in a mixture of notes and coinage so that it can be easily split into three. Loose change is a very definite requirement of *The Pocket Money Plan*.

Give your child cash for as long as it's possible (and safe) to do so. As they get older (say beyond 11) there may be larger sums involved, which can move their financial education onto sensible use of cash machines and debit cards.

Before then children need the experience of handling cash. When they are young, it's the only way to find out what the notes and coins look like. But the main benefit is to learn what parting with their hard-earned cash feels like – and to realise how traumatic it can sometimes feel. Only the Tooth Fairy and Father Christmas can make money appear by magic. For everything else, cash is required. Our children need to know this.

HELPFUL IDEAS
CASH FOR THE WEEK

As adults, we are so used to paying with plastic or standing orders that we've forgotten how it feels to spend cash. I'll set you a challenge. Use nothing but cash for a week. You'll regain an appreciation of how quickly it disappears, and be much more aware of the amount you spend. What's more, your children will see you using cash and follow your example.

HOW TO TURN YOUR 'STUFF' SPEND INTO THE POCKET MONEY PLAN

EXAMPLE 1

Fred is 8 years old. He plays footy after school twice a week, and is learning the guitar.

Step 1: Analyse the spend

For three months, Fred's Mum writes down everything she spends on her darling boy. She finds that this comes to £120.

She's been careful to ensure her calculations give a true picture. The three months included a half term holiday, so she can see the effect of extra spending when Fred isn't at school. She's also taken into account that there weren't any important events such as a family holiday or Christmas.

Step 2: Check it's affordable

Fred's Mum has a really good think about whether £120 is affordable, bearing in mind the overall financial circumstances of her family. If it is, great. If not, she needs to look at what a more realistic amount would be.

Step 3: Who buys what

Next she works out what outlay she is going to keep funding, and

The Pocket Money Plan

what Fred is going to be responsible for. With Fred, she agrees that he will now buy his own sweets, drinks, and comics – about £3 a week. Meanwhile, mum continues paying for everything else: family outings, essential clothes, football club fees and kit, guitar lessons/equipment and Xmas presents.

Step 4: Calculate The Pocket Money Plan spend

Fred's Mum decides what giving, saving and spending formula she wants to employ. She settles on 10, 30 and 60 per cent. So here's how she calculates Fred's weekly pocket money.

Money needed for Fred's stuff = £3

Spend fund = 60 per cent of The Pocket Money Plan budget

So 10 per cent is one sixth of £3 – ie 50p.

This means:

Money needed for Giving (10 per cent) = 50p

Money needed for Saving (30 per cent) = £1.50

Money needed for Fred's Pocket Money Plan = £5.00 per week

EXAMPLE 2

Sonia is 14. She's an ace hockey player and loves going out with her friends.

Step 1: Analyse the spend

Sonia's Dad undertakes the same exercise as Fred's Mum. 'Stuff' analysis for Sonia shows that she's spent £420 over three months. This period included Christmas and there were lots of social events.

Step 2: Check it's affordable

Dad has to decide if this is affordable bearing in mind his financial situation. Perhaps Sonia should contribute something towards her lifestyle by finding a Saturday job.

Step 3: Who buys what

Dad decides that he will continue to buy: family outings, essential clothes, hockey equipment and fees.

Sonia will now buy: her own sweets, drinks, cinema tickets, magazines, fashion clothes, music, make-up, jewellery, Xmas and birthday presents for friends and family.

Looking at the 'stuff' it is clear that a lot is being spent on clothes and make up. Dad reckons that his spend on the essentials is around £60 per month while Sonia's 'stuff' is costing £80 per month.

Sonia's Dad decides that the stuff budget should be less than is currently being spent. They need to have a talk about whether Sonia

The Pocket Money Plan

will try to be a bit more economical or whether she will help out by getting a job.

Step 4: Calculate The Pocket Money Plan spend

Sonia's Dad decides on the 10/30/60 formula for giving, saving and spending.

Money allocated for Sonia's stuff = £60 per month

If Spend fund = 60% of Pocket Money Plan budget, this means that

Money needed for Giving (10 per cent) = £10

Money needed for Saving (30 per cent) = £30

Money needed for Sonia's Pocket Money Plan = £100.00 per month

We should note that in this example Sonia's Dad doesn't pay more under *The Pocket Money Plan*. He moves around his resources to teach some valuable money lessons. If Sonia wants to keep her current lifestyle she has some thinking to do about how she might afford it! Luckily, *The Pocket Money Plan* has plenty of ideas to help her.

STEP 5
LINK POCKET MONEY
TO 'EARNING'

So far your child has had the chance to learn to manage his or her money well. The next stage is to show that the stuff doesn't grow on trees. Instead, he has to work for it.

Yes, even for pocket money. By earning it himself your child will begin, perhaps for the first time, to realise what money is really worth. This 'eureka moment' is crucial. Little that's worthwhile in this life comes easily. As parents we know that if we strive really hard for something it often means a great deal to us. In this section of *The Pocket Money Plan* your child will discover this too.

Don't feel that it's too early to teach your child this way of thinking. Research shows that the home is where children learn the benefits of hard work, just as it shows that families with no 'worker', or families with debt problems, produce children less likely to get a job.

So how does your child earn pocket money? With nothing more than good behaviour and a few basic tasks. Many of them will be things you already encourage your child to do – but now there is an extra incentive to do them! This isn't about creating the perfect child; it's just about encouraging his or her responsibility as one of the family to perform certain tasks and behave in certain ways. In return, your child receives pocket money, and the chance to spend most of it exactly as he or she chooses. Over time your child will also discover the pride that comes from earning, and a sense of how valuable money can be.

The commonest way to keep track of the behaviours (see list opposite) is the classic 'star chart', or list on the fridge door. You can download a very useful one from www.pocketmoneyplan. co.uk, or even buy a posh laminated version. It really depends on how regimented you want to be. Once you're a seasoned Pocket Money Planner you may well dispense with a list altogether, or reintroduce a modified version if behaviour is slipping. The main thing is to be flexible. Find the way that works for you.

Of course there will come a time when your child doesn't behave. Under no circumstances fall into the trap of threatening to cut pocket money. Nothing will switch a child off *The Pocket Money Plan* faster than if it becomes just another way to nag. Instead, either introduce extra tasks for the same 'wage', or ban extra earnings for a while (Step 6).

HELPFUL IDEAS
HOW TO EARN POCKET MONEY

This list gives some ideas for the tasks and behaviours which you can link to weekly payment of pocket money. The final selection is up to you, based on the minimum you need your child to achieve to meet her responsibilities as part of the family. When you've selected a final list, write it down and agree it with your child, including penalties for non-compliance.

● Get out of bed (teenagers)

● Stay in bed/quietly in bedroom until a civilised hour (small children)

● Make the bed/tidy bedroom (to your standards)

● Brush teeth without being reminded

● Prepare own school snacks (healthy choices could earn extra reward)

● Put only dirty clothes in the dirty washing basket

The Pocket Money Plan

- Get dressed when asked
- Wash (always a good one, this)
- Change underwear (especially boys)
- Remember school equipment before leaving the house
- Put toys away
- Set the table
- Practise musical instrument regularly
- Make mum tea (sheer bliss)
- Do homework before asking for TV/DVD/computer
- Stop/start when asked
- Be kind to brothers and sisters (or at least pretend)
- Use good table manners
- Go to bed without an argument
- Do what he knows he should, without being asked
- Be polite
- Do what you tell them
- Be respectful to their elders

A MODERN TALE

The scene: a sofa on a recent series of the tv show *Big Brother*. In a normal conversation one of the contestants reveals to a fellow housemate that she wasn't meant to be poor. Indeed, she hates it, and she can't stand it much longer. So she has a plan: she is going to be a footballer's wife.

Let's unpick that. First of all, she clearly isn't really poor. Secondly, what has she done about her situation? Gone to college or university to get a practical qualification? Worked in a job (or maybe two at once) where there was career progression? Saved some of her meagre earnings to build for the future?

Apparently not. Instead, she auditions for *Big Brother* and tells the whole world (or the bit of it tuned in at the time) that she's going to marry someone rich.

Is this really the money message we want our children to hear?

STEP 6
ENCOURAGE EXTRA EARNING

The harder you work, as a general rule, the richer you become. The earlier your child can begin to understand this concept the better. Everywhere they see examples of wealthy sportsmen and women, or pop stars, who apparently haven't worked very hard to gain their riches. But of course most of these 'stars' have worked extremely hard to get where they are – and even then they are one of a very, very few lucky individuals.

Your child can't grow up relying on luck to deliver financial security. That's why *The Pocket Money Plan* encourages a desire to earn more than his or her regular allowance. Your child needs to realise that the only way to get what they want is to work for it – whether we're talking about money or anything else he or she might want to achieve.

WHEN IT'S HIS IDEA

Once your child gets a taste for earning, he or she will almost certainly want more. And the first person to be asked will be you. That's a good sign, but children need to understand three things:
1. Money is a limited resource

2. You are paying your child to do extra chores which you would otherwise do yourself – so you are doing your child a favour, just as much as he or she is helping you.

3. Your child is just one of a family. You only have a set income, and it has to be distributed fairly amongst all of you.

For these reasons, encourage children to come to you with a good proposal. Only fund additional chores if there is a particular goal in mind – for example, a special piece of sports equipment, extra funds for a holiday, or a gift for another person. If you feel your child is old enough, the work is appropriate, and you can afford to reward it, then go ahead. The underlying aim is to let your child earn more if he or she wants to, but on your terms.

These terms apply also when children are working for friends or family, too.

WHEN IT'S YOUR IDEA

There will always be some items and activities which, in the pre-*Pocket Money Plan* days, you would have funded. They tend to be real treats particular to your child, rather than the family as a whole. Now you have a strategy to deal with money education, think about getting your child to help you to meet these expenses by extra earning. This has two benefits. First, it reinforces the idea that money can be hard to come by. Second, it encourages your child to consider the impact on the family's total budget. Third, it helps you gauge how desirable the item in question really is. If your son and daughter isn't willing to devote time and energy to help pay for it, then maybe he doesn't want it that much after all.

LET'S TAKE AN EXAMPLE

Twelve year-old Simon is desperate to go on a school ski trip to Austria next year. All his friends are signed up, and it's clear he will have a fantastic experience. But it's a week-long trip, and the school is asking for £550 – enough to buy a week's camping and surfing for the whole family. His mum discusses this with him. He isn't being mean or inappropriate; he needs some sense of what the trip really costs.

She strikes a deal. She'll pay 90 per cent and he will earn the final 10 per cent from doing jobs. They agree a list of chores.

Simon not only rises to the challenge, but sets himself an objective of his own by earning an extra £10 as pocket money for the trip. He comes back tired, smelly and happy. What did he spend the money on? He bought his brother a teddy bear, his sister some soap and himself some disgusting sugary drinks that mum would never have allowed. His mum got nothing, but that didn't stop him making her very, very proud.

In fact, it's a true story. Would he have appreciated the trip quite as much if his parents had simply written the cheque and handed him a tenner? I think not.

EXTRA EARNING IDEAS

- Gardening
- Cleaning (kids are rubbish at it but some help is better than none)
- Dusting (my five year-old actually likes it, but then I'm not a fan of fine china)
- Cooking for the family (older children)
- Helping prepare a meal (younger children)
- Car washing (although they will miss bits)
- Sock pairing
- Helping younger ones with homework
- Looking after or babysitting younger siblings
- Taking responsibility for the family pet
- Vacuuming
- Loading/unloading the dishwasher

Remember you don't pay your child for anything he or she should do as part of the family. You reward these baseline activities with the normal Pocket Money allowance.

HOW MUCH TO PAY?

This is a preparation for the real world, so be realistic. I pay the minimum wage (currently £3 an hour for over 16s – below that there's no legal figure) according to the time it should take to complete the task – which is not the same as the time it actually takes. If it's a hard job, such as raking leaves in cold weather, I might offer a bit more. If it's extremely easy or almost a basic activity, I pay a little less.

SHOULD EXTRA EARNED MONEY BE FOR GIVING AND SAVING TOO?

This is something to discuss up-front with your child. Once you've established a proportional split for Pocket Money I would strongly suggest that it applies to extra earned money too. It is extremely important for your child to accept as the norm that there are other calls on his funds before spending. This is the strategy you want him to adopt as an adult.

THE LAW ON CHILDREN WORKING

Gone are the days when you could send your kids up a chimney to earn an honest crust. Today there are over 200 pieces of legislation, ranging from European Laws and Acts of Parliament to local authority by-laws, which govern when and where children aged under 16 are employed. If your child is working to earn extra money you need to bear these in mind. Earning extra is a great idea – but only in moderation

Mostly, though, it is the Children and Young Persons Act 1933 which sets out the rules. The nitty-gritty is this:

1) Children cannot work before they are 13, although a local authority can give special permission if the work is for a performance, modelling or sport.

2) When they reach 14 they can work five hours on a Saturday and in the holidays, but never more than 25 hours per week. At 15+ it's eight hours on Saturdays and 35 hours a week overall.

3) During term time they cannot work for more that 12 hours a week or for more than two hours on a school day, or a Sunday.

4) All children must be given at least a two week break from work during school holidays

5) Children can never work before 7am or after 7pm, and can't work in betting shops and petrol stations. Street-trading and selling

scrap metals are also no-nos. Performing abroad is only allowed with a special licence. In general, the tasks should be 'light work'. Working conditions should not be harmful to their safety, health or development, and should not compromise their education.

6) The minimum wage does not apply to under 16s, and for 16 and 17 year-olds it's £3 per hour. I'd suggest that anything less than this, for anyone, is an insult!

WHEN TO INTRODUCE THE POCKET MONEY PLAN?

Ideally, start giving your child pocket money as soon as he or she understands the concept of handing over cash to buy something. Generally this happens around age five. This is also the time when basic arithmetic will be kicking in. As long as a child knows that, if there are two chocolate bars and one is eaten then one is left, then it's time to start. However, if your child is already older than this, start anyway. Children of any age, and adults too, will benefit from the Plan's six steps. Please don't expect instant results. Your child will not learn money management overnight. You are trying to instil a way of managing money that will be used into adulthood, and that takes time. And on that basis, the sooner you start the better.

WHAT ABOUT MONEY GIFTS?

Friends and relations will often give money at birthdays, Christmas, and other times too. Should it become part of *The Pocket Money Plan*, with some set aside for Giving and Saving before the remainder is spent?

I think it depends. By all means tell grandparents, aunts and uncles about the strategy you have adopted for teaching your kids about money. They will almost certainly be impressed. But you can't impose *The Pocket Money Plan* on them. If they've given the money for your child to buy something specific you have to respect their wishes. A half-way solution is to negotiate a smaller Giving and Saving proportion that usual, depending on how much wonga your little devil manages to amass!

Grandparents in particular are usually all for Saving, often having grown up in a time when credit was never freely available, and when people bought only what they could afford. Some grandparents may have experienced rationing after the Second World War, and may remember their own parents splitting money up on a weekly basis just as you are teaching your child to do now. If that's the case, your child's grandparents could become your greatest Pocket Money Plan allies.

We make a living
by what we get,
but we make a life by
what we give

WINSTON CHURCHILL

CHAPTER TWO

GIVING

f all the ideas in this book, Giving is the most controversial.

'We can't afford to give to charity.'

'Charity begins at home.'

'Are you mad?'

These are understandable reactions, but hear me out. Asking your child to set some pocket money aside for charity is more than just an altruistic exercise. It is, in fact, the best way to help your child learn how to manage his or her money.

HOW GIVING HELPS YOUR CHILD LEARN

The first lesson that Giving teaches has nothing to do with good causes. It introduces children to the idea that when they get older, and have to stand on their own two feet, they will never be able to spend all of their money as they choose. We adults have liabilities to meet each month, regardless of whether we want to pay for them. The minute our salaries hit the bank account, there are

those little devils (or direct debits) ready to pounce.

If we give children regular pocket money to spend entirely as they wish, we are failing to teach them how the real world works. Giving creates for your child a 'bill' – a weekly or monthly commitment that must be met before the 'me money' becomes available.

This ability to ensure we have enough to fund our social lives, as well as to pay the bills, is called budgeting. We'll come back to it in Chapter 7, but for now it's enough to recognise that it's a crucial money management skill, and one where the majority of people fall down. Introducing your child to the discipline of Giving helps ensure he or she won't make those mistakes.

SOMEONE OTHER THAN ME, ME, ME

Children today have become very used to 'getting'. The days are long gone when Christmas was about a few marbles and a shiny red apple in the heel of an old sock. Now it's about electronic toys, wads of cash and a sackload of booty. Birthdays, even for the young, rarely involve the simple celebrations of old. Pass the parcel and a few sausage rolls have been replaced by a visit to a theme park. And, when the sun has set on yet another action-packed birthday adventure, a slice of iced sponge will no longer do as a parting gift. Instead, mothers stay awake worrying about the contents of the dreaded party bag and its acceptability to a bunch of demanding six-year-olds.

This tendency to over-consume only increases as children enter their teens. Research from Cornhill Direct claims that the average teenager is walking out the door for an evening with around £700 of clothing and gadgets, plus a further £30 for spending.

The fact is that many children get too much, and we are setting them up for a fall if we do not do something about this. By introducing the concept of Giving, *The Pocket Money Plan* shifts the focus away from 'me', shows them they have enough 'stuff', and gets them thinking about the world around them.

GROWING RESPONSIBILITY

Of course the image of the pampered young Western consumer is not the full story. Children instinctively have a sense of responsibility for their position in the world. When asked, most of them wish for a world where everyone is safe and has enough to eat. They know they are lucky in comparison to others, and often understand why.

Studies by the Citizenship Foundation found that 78 per cent of children who had given money to charity felt good about themselves, while 89 per cent of children thought that giving to charity was a good thing. A similar number felt that giving a little bit of regular income to charity was something everyone ought to do.

As a parent you can use these facts to link your child's sense of responsibility to his or hers money box. But that responsibility must never become guilt. The Pocket Money Plan's Give, Save, Spend formula should prevent this, but make sure your child doesn't use some of the

spend fund for Giving. Your child cannot take the cares of the world onto his shoulders. Once your child knows that you and they have a responsibility to give a little, he or she is perfectly entitled to enjoy the remainder.

EXPERIENCE, NOT LECTURES

Parents often resort to lectures when trying to teach children the value of money, but lectures are not fun for children – or, for that matter, adults. A good charity, which your child really cares about, and which delivers results, will demonstrate that value far more powerfully, and on your child's terms.

Whether it be feeding a child thousands of miles away, helping save an animal from extinction, or funding a tiny step in the long journey to find a cure for a disease, your child's money will have an impact. Raise him with the notion of how satisfying this is, and maybe the balance of power will start to swing away from the 'Want it? Gotta have it!' marketeers.

ONE EXAMPLE OF GIVING

The Smith family (mum, dad and three kids) sponsor a little girl in Cambodia called Sarang through World Vision. They pay for her schooling and contribute towards basic amenities in the village where she lives. Sarang doesn't have much, and the letters they receive from Cambodia remind them of this.

The family funds the £10 cost of supporting Sarang together. Mum and dad pay six months' subscription; the children fund the rest by paying two months each. One month comes out of their Christmas money, the other from their birthday money. They don't begrudge it because the setup is real: they have a stake in the life of a child who needs their help. And that connection has developed because they are supporting her with their own money.

HOW TO CHOOSE A CHARITY

Start with a discussion. Whether you mean it to or not, it will revolve around your child's values. Normally such a conversation is bewildering for a child, but if you ask your child where he or she wants to splash the cash to help others he or she will have a thousand ideas. Explain what choices say about the kind of person your child is, and watch him or her grow with pride.

Your child might show generosity by wanting to help a whole host of people; compassion as he or she finds someone less fortunate than themself to support; integrity as he or she stands up for what he or she believes in; or courage if he or she chooses an unpopular cause. Whatever his or her ideas, *The Pocket Money Plan* is allowing your child, and you, to discover all of these great things about themself.

Help your child narrow choices down to a couple of broad issues to be supported – for example, conservation or child poverty. Next, ask whether he or she would like to help these causes on a worldwide basis or just in the UK. Research has found that children are hugely influenced by their parents, particularly their mothers, when they give to charity. Nevertheless your child may want to help a different cause. Try not to guide them too much, and, as long as your child can explain why it is important to him or her, then offer your backing.

CHARITY TIPS FOR CHILDREN

CHECK THE TERMINOLOGY

The Citizenship Foundation has found that young children sometimes confuse 'charities' with 'people who ask you for money'. Your child may not yet understand that charities do something useful with the money after you give it to them.

MAKE IT REAL

Give your child a clear idea of what he or she has funded. 'You gave money to pay for an operation to save someone's sight in Africa,' is much easier to relate to than– 'You gave £10 to charity.'

CHOOSE A TALKATIVE CHARITY

Most charities send regular updates to supporters, and these are really important for your child. They're a chance for children to stay connected to what their money is achieving, as well as the charity's wider work. Really small charities may not have much money for communications, but if you explain that the donation comes from a young child they will almost certainly make an exception.

FOCUS ON THE POSITIVE

Concepts such as famine and AIDS aren't always easy to explain to a young child, and deciding the right age is up to you. Meanwhile it might be easier to introduce the charities who keep us safe or make the world a nicer place, such the St John's Ambulance, the RNLI or the National Trust.

MAXIMISE THE BENEFIT

For any charity, two pounds a month is far better than a £100 windfall. Not only does it allow them to plan ahead, but your child's regular donation can then attract Gift Aid, which increases the value of every contribution. Gift Aid is tax relief on money donated to UK charities. Donations are treated as if the basic rate tax has already been deducted. The charity can then reclaim this tax to increase the value of the donation.

Gift Aid only applies if you've paid enough income and/or capital

gains tax to cover what the charity will reclaim. For that reason you need to give the money in your name, rather than that of your child. To set up Gift Aid you can fill out a short form, usually supplied by the charity.

ABOVE ALL...

Choosing a charity with your child should be fun, not a guilt trip. There is no place here for 'Think of the starving children in Africa' lectures. Instead, the aim is to get your child to take delight in discovering how the power of money can help others – and practice managing it at the same time.

WWW.GUIDESTAR.ORG

This handy website helps narrow down your choices by searching all UK charities in a chosen field. It also gives you access to Annual Trustees' Reports, which show how much the charity is spending on administration in relation to how much it is raising.

OTHER WAYS TO GIVE

In terms of self-worth, giving without using money can still count towards the total in your child's Giving pot. One example is donating an old toy to a charity shop. Let your child take the item into the shop and ask how much it might be sold for. Then you can note the amount and add it to the Giving pot.

Another option, especially for teenagers, might be giving time – perhaps an hour a week to help an old neighbour, or through the national scheme run by Age Concern. The volunteering website www.do-it.org.uk holds a register of all the UK organisations looking for volunteers. Work like this doesn't half look good on a cv.

Of course your child's Giving money needn't only go to a charity. It can be used for simple acts of kindness – a get well card or treat for an unwell friend, or a bunch of flowers for a neighbour whose pet has just died. Even planting a tree or putting up a feeder for the birds in the garden is a form of Giving. It all helps instil good money management, as well as good values.

A FRIEND IN NEED

Harry had been playing rugby for four years before he became the first major injury on the team, with a broken collarbone. All his mates were upset, and worried that he was in pain. Steve wanted to cheer his friend up, so he went to his Give jar and bought Harry an enormous bar of chocolate and a copy of Rugby World. He posted the goodies to his friend's house with a get well soon note. The next day Harry called to say thanks.

It was a slightly different approach to Giving, but in *Pocket Money Plan* terms Steve was showing the same decision-making money skills as giving to charity. And of course both lads felt good about it too.

> "We are what we repeatedly do. Excellence, then, is not an act but a habit.
>
> ARISTOTLE

"Those are my saving account managers."

CHAPTER
THREE

SAVING

If there's one instinct no child is born with, it's saving. Delaying spending money until some point in the future comes about as easily to a young mind as losing a limb. How much more fun to throw caution to the wind, and spend like there's no tomorrow!

And yet tomorrow always comes – and life teaches us that it will be just as expensive as today.

Children don't know this yet. So it's our job to break it to them, gently. Because saving is probably the most important financial skill anyone can ever learn.

So if you are going to be successful in turning your child into a willing saver, you need help. And that is what this chapter is about: to reach a point with your child where the desire to win the end game outweighs his or her need for an immediate result.

SAVING IS A HABIT

If saving came as naturally as breathing, we'd all be doing it. Yet, over half of British adults don't save. It's too boring. It takes too

long. Our debt statistics are the result!

So saving is one of the habits your child needs to develop whilst still young. Recognise this and you're half way there. It really is no different from your child learning to say 'please' and 'thank you' – in fact it might take just as long to get established. But once the habit forms then, like the ability to be polite, it will stand your child in good stead for the rest of his life.

SO WHY TEACH IT IN THE FIRST PLACE?

One simple reason: financial security. That means the ability to deal with the unexpected. Having to hand the right resources to deal with life as it snaps at our heels. It's something we all want for ourselves, and for our children. Without savings to call upon, our financial security, to be frank, is on rocky ground.

In fact, the benefits of saving stretch far beyond the material. Many studies show how financial security is good for us psychologically – that it's better for our health and our happiness if we have some money put by. It can give us the ability to sleep at night, or the luxury of choices when the road ahead is uncertain. It can allow us to take a calculated risk when another person has no option but to proceed with caution. It can provide a springboard for change, or the opportunity to switch to plan B when things go wrong.

No one should ever fall into the trap of believing that money is everything, but it does help. If you don't have enough savings yourself (or can remember a time when you didn't), imagine how much easier life would be right now with a little nest egg you could call upon when times get tough.

And from your point of view as a mum or dad reading this book, think of the saving habit as a loving gift to your child to help him when he finally sets off into the big, bad world on his own – a financial cushion there to catch him if he should fall. What parent wouldn't want that?

But this is all grown-up stuff. How do you begin to tell your child about it? Well, first you must create the right atmosphere – so start talking to him about your life. You are his first and best role model, and almost every day throws up a chance to show how your savings (or lack of them) help or get in the way. There are two main ways to do this.

1) TELL THEM WHEN YOU USE YOUR SAVINGS

Suppose the washing machine breaks down. If you run to the nearest electrical store and replace it with a new model, without explaining how it's being paid for, you simply reinforce the 'money grows on trees' theory. Your child needs to know that you can only buy new things at a moment's notice because you have savings. If you have no savings, and need to use credit, maybe he needs to know this too.

The rule is: if you have to dip into the pot for something unforseen, tell him! Not only will he learn the value of saving; he'll appreciate the item your frugality has paid for.

2) TELL THEM WHEN YOU ARE SAVING FOR SOMETHING

I often tell my children that we are on an economy drive (we are on one at the moment, actually). They need to know that there is no shame in this.

We have a holiday in six weeks (whoopee)! The holiday is paid for, but I'm saving for spending money. So it's no eating out, no takeaways, and be more frugal than usual at the supermarket. The children know about this, and they know why. When we eventually go on holiday they will see the value of my savings – that the financial cushion I made over the last few months had positive benefits.

Every family can find dozens of examples like this. Involve your child, and he or she will learn.

LIFE IS EXPENSIVE!

Cost today	Estimated cost in 5 years

● Deposit on a house: first time buyer

£15,157	£17,100

Halifax average house price of first time buyer property for December 2006 of £151,565.

● Wedding

£19,300	£21,800

Information via email from the PR Manager at Confetti and cost includes honeymoon

● Gap year travel

£12,377	£14,000

Based on a non-working trip. Airfare for a round-the-world ticket lasting 364 days from Travel Insurance from www.statravel.co.uk assuming inflation at 2.5 % a year (July 05).

● Hajj or Umrah Trip

£2,750	£3,110

Based on a non-working trip. Includes return airfares from London, 3/4 Star accommodation assuming inflation at 2.5% a year.

● University course

£40,400	£45,822

Based on average cost of three-year course outside London. Source: the children's Mutual.

Estimated cost in 12 years	Estimated cost in 15 years	Estimated cost in 18 years
£20,300	**£21,900**	**£23,600**
Assuming inflation at 2.5% a year (December 2006).		
£25,900	**£27,900**	**£30,100**
assuming inflation at 2.5% a year (July 2007).		
£16,600	**£17,900**	**£19,300**
www.statravel.co.uk. Daily living costs from Lonely Planet Publications.		
£3,690	**£3,980**	**£4,280**
at double occupancy, transfers and meals from www.haj.co.uk (July 2007)		
£54,467	**£58,656**	**£63,166**
Assuming inflation at 2.5% a year (July 2008).		

Everyone has different priorities, but whichever your child chooses they're going to cost you. Fortunately *The Pocket Money Plan* can help. Few of us are in a position to fund any of these big events, but we can still save a little towards the most important ones – the book fund for university, the hostel fees for the round-the-world-trip, the insurance for the first car, the champagne for the wedding. All it takes is a plan. Then, when the financial burden finally falls on your shoulders, it will at least be a little easier to bear.

THREE STEPS TO TEACH YOUR CHILD TO SAVE

The Pocket Money Plan introduces saving to your child by asking him or her to set aside a fixed slice of the weekly allowance. It's the regularity of splitting money like this – week in, week out – that matters. Keep at it and, one day, it will turn into a habit.

The beauty of this system is that it gets things in the right order: you save before you spend. Saving just doesn't happen if it's something you do with the money you have left. There never is any left! So, the rule is short and sweet:

1. Put some money aside every week for saving;

2. Do this before you spend any money.

This is the foundation you're building on. Get it right, and the rest is just re-inforcement.

1. MAKE A FUSS

By hook or by crook, you've got to find some way to make this saving malarkey exciting. Again, I'll suggest that a new money box is a good idea, and three separate money pots are ideal. But why not open a new bank or building society account for your child (see chapter 4 for how to choose a good one)? Involve him or her in the selection process and the visit to deal with the paperwork.

If funds allow, give your child an introductory bonus, perhaps equivalent to his first deposit, and returnable if further deposits aren't made at the agreed times. Another ruse is to offer a list of tasks you are prepared to pay for during the few days before you open the account, to give the savings a head start.

2. KEEP THE MONEY VISIBLE

When adults save, the money doesn't (unless we are extremely unlucky) disappear into a black hole. You child doesn't know this, so make sure the money pots aren't hidden away. Having them close by allows you to discuss them more too. When you move onto banks and other forms of saving, choose a company willing to interact with your child. Every piece of information that comes through the door is a chance for a chat – and a little bit of learning.

If you are brave enough, lead by example and get some money pots of your own!

3. SET EXCITING OBJECTIVES

Forget about saving for a rainy day for the moment: children (and adults) respond better to positives. This is your child's 'me' money for the future, and within reason you can let your child's mind run riot about what to spend it on.

So what does your child want to spend it on? Once there's a decision, your child has an objective – and that allows him or her to see what the aim is, and when it's to be achieved. Your child's aims may well change along the way, but starting out with a living, breathing goal is an absolute must.

CHILDREN AGED 5-14

For younger children, short-term aims are the only ones that make sense. It is unreasonable and unrealistic to expect anything else. 'When I am older', for a five year-old, is five and a half! So focus on short, sharp experiences of the winning feeling that saving for something can bring.

Usually this means 'stuff' which, in pre-Pocket Money Plan days, you would have bought for your child anyway. Saving for these things, in a fairly short time period, satisfies your child's need for instant gratification, at least to some extent. But at the same time he gets the satisfaction of having done it on his or her own.

If children struggle with the concept of saving, try a sliding scale

of short-term goals. Let children save for a month and, when that works, set another slightly longer time frame, and so on. Before long your child's patience will develop on discovering that good things come to those who wait.

CHILDREN AGED 14+

As children get older, concepts like 'when I go to uni' and 'when I'm old enough to drive' get more concrete. So it's important now to set at least some longer-term objectives. And, at some point, just setting aside a fixed proportion of pocket money won't be enough. Just where is the money for that gap year going to come from? Perhaps other members of the family step in to help, or your child takes a job in his spare time.

Longer-term objectives are a huge help in getting your child to begin taking some responsibility for his future. Eventually, your child will learn that planning ahead gives choices that wouldn't otherwise occur.

THE S.M.A.R.T. WAY TO SET SAVINGS OBJECTIVES

The SMART method of setting goals is widely used in business. It gives a logical framework that allows us to define what we want to achieve. It's also another chance to discuss a responsible approach to money with your child.

S IS FOR SPECIFIC

Your children need to know very precisely what they are aiming for. Without that defined goal, they won't grasp the purpose of saving rather than spending. At best, children will find it hard to get excited. At worst, they'll give up.

The thought process goes like this.

1) Jack is saving for Christmas.

(but what exactly is it about Christmas that he is saving for?)

2) Jack is saving enough to buy a gift for his sister and brother.

(Be even more specific.)

3) Jack would like to buy his sister a book and his brother a new teddy bear.

Ok, we got there!

The more long-term the savings period, the more specific you need to be. I've lost count of the number of parents who say they're, 'saving for when their children are older'. What age do the children need to be before they get their hands on the loot? 16? 18? 25? And when they have waited patiently for this indeterminate time period, what are they to do with the money?

Don't try this approach, especially with teenagers: it just won't work. In fact, don't try it on yourself either. It's extremely difficult to get excited about the future prospect of achieving something when you haven't a clue what it is.

Of course, the objective can always change. For example, you may decide with your child that you will save together for a second

hand car when he is 18. This is specific, and also something he or she can get a warm feeling about. If your child gets to 18 and you agree the money can be spent on something else, then at least the money is there to decide about.

KEEP THE SAVE POT FOR SAVING

If you're not careful, your child might use the short-term savings to fund the things that really should be coming out of the Spending pot (see Spending section, chapter 7). The basic idea is that short-term goals should fund one-off items, not something that is (or could be) a regular buy.

So it's fine for your child to use the Save fund for a computer game, but not to buy the book he or she should have been able to afford a few weeks ago, but couldn't because the wonga had been spent sweets.

The same applies to events. While it is OK to set a savings goal for a school trip or to have extra holiday money, it is not OK for a teenager to 'save' for the 30th trip to the cinema this summer.

The main thing is to always know where you're going. If at all possible, keep a picture of the thing or event your child is aiming for next to the pocket money pots.

M IS FOR MEASURABLE

If we go back to Jack, who wants to buy a book and a teddy bear as Christmas presents, making his objective measurable means him working out what his festive generosity is going to cost him. Without this vital detail the whole plan could go out of the window at any moment. Equally, for the long-term aim of a second hand car, we need a ballpark figure in mind.

	First new car www.whatcar.co.uk. E.g Daihatsu Charade, Fiat Panda and Citroen C1, £8,230. Assumes inflation at 2.5% a year (July 07).	**Secondhand car** www.whatcar.co.uk. A typical 5-year old second hand car. E.g 2002 Fiat Punto Hatchback 1.2 3dr cost £2,825(July 07). Assumes inflation at 2.5% a year.
Cost today	**£8,247**	**£2,825**
Estimated cost in 5 year	**£9,330**	**£3,190**
Estimated cost in 12 years	**£11,000**	**£3,790**
Estimated cost in 15 years	**£11,900**	**£4,090**
Estimated cost in 18 years	**£12,800**	**£4,090**

Source: Childrens Mutual

A IS FOR APPROPRIATE

Children are children, and teenagers are, by and large, a law unto themselves. But there is little point in either of them latching onto an objective which you won't allow.

Appropriate stands for other things too. Sometimes, your child will have short-term and long-term objectives running alongside each other. You need to check that they are balanced appropriately.

The same goes for spending those savings. If Jack has had a picture of a computer game next to his Savings pot, don't let him bin it so that he can afford to buy that book and teddy. He needs to know that it's not appropriate to forego his own objectives to replace them with those of others.

But this is easier to deal with than the child who carefully saves for his own short-term objectives but then tries to finance Christmas from his Spending pot (or, even worse, Giving pot). Don't allow this! You have to be cruel to be kind.

R IS FOR REALISTIC

In other words, can your child afford it?

Jack needs to know that, on £4 a week, the book for his sister isn't going to be a first edition and his brother's teddy won't be made by Stieff. Equally, your teenager's car is likely to be a fairly humble model.

Best, then, to manage the expectations now – and make triple sure you aren't setting your child up to fall even as he or she sets out on this whole money management mission. Help him set goals that are within reach. That way your child won't see saving as a burden, but as a way to realize his or her dreams.

T IS FOR TIMED

Imagine getting up on Monday and not knowing when Friday was going to come. It's no different with saving: you have to tie childrens objectives to a time scale which you, and they,

TOP TIP: MAKE A MONEY MONITOR

£14
£12
£10
£8
£6
£4
£2

We've all seen the 'appeal progress' charts (usually in the shape of a thermometer) outside a church with a leaky roof. Why not make one to help your child understand how far he has to go to before he reaches her objective?

It's ideal for short-term goals, and if your child is older you can even use it for long-term ones too. Kept beside her money pots and picture, a money monitor is all the motivation he'll need.

understand from the outset.

Long-term time scales depend either on a life event ('when I'm 18'), or something like Christmas or the family holiday. Either way, the trick is to make sure the budget matches the time available. And that in turn means that Jack needs to understand when to start saving for his brother and sister's presents. Equally, if your 14 year-old thinks he can save enough to buy a decent car for when he passes his test, he'd better get his skates on and find some extra earnings pronto.

It's a good idea with long-term goals to take into account the effect of inflation, and any interest or growth on your child's money if it's saved or invested. You can find a convenient calculator for this on www.pocketmoneyplan.co.uk.

If your child has a goal in mind, but is in no particular hurry to achieve it, then you can let the budget dictate the time frame like this:

- Amount I can afford each week for this savings goal **£1**
- Amount needed **£10**
- Weeks to reach my goal **10 weeks**

It's not that complicated, but it's still a valuable lesson for your child. And during the process a surprising thing may happen. Your child may decide that the item isn't wanted after all. It might be one of those things that, in pre-Pocket Money Plan days, you might have bought immediately. Now that your child's having to save for it, it's not quite so attractive. Funny that.

COULD GRANDPARENTS HELP?

You may be pleasantly surprised by offers of help, particularly from grandparents, once word gets out that you have specific plans in place. Often I have advised clients who would love to contribute to their grandchildren's future, but hold back. Their main reasons are offending their children (!), or worries that the grandchildren will 'blow the lot' on frivolous expenditure. I have lost count of the number of grandparents who want to put in place measures to control how savings for grandchildren are spent. To my mind, this is a little like baking a cake and asking them not to eat it.

The Pocket Money Plan, with its emphasis on saving objectives and good financial discipline, is often all the reassurance a concerned grandparent needs to help build that financial cushion we all want our children to have.

WHY GRANDPARENTS SAVE FOR THEIR GRANDCHILDREN

1. Concerns about rising property prices **31 per cent**

2. To fund grandchildren's education **25 per cent**

3. To help them onto the property ladder **17 per cent**

4. Concerns that the child will have a lower quality of life than they did **13 per cent**

5. Worries that parents can't provide for their children **11 per cent**

Source : CreditExpert.co.uk

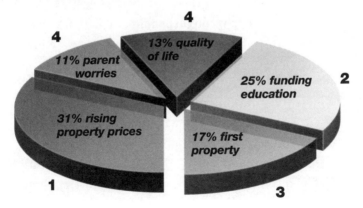

IF YOU IGNORE EVERYTHING ELSE IN THIS BOOK

Get your child into the habit of saving. The goals and the things you're aiming to buy don't really matter; they're just the means by which you establish the habit. What counts is the habit.

You may not be able to give as much for your child's Save pot as you feel you should – but give it anyway! Never be fooled into thinking (as so many people are) that if you can't afford to save something substantial then there is no point. This is absolute rubbish. Over a long term, even a small amount of money saved can add up.

The reason? Compound interest.

THE MIRACLE OF COMPOUND INTEREST

Albert Einstein once described compound interest as a miracle. On another occasion he named it, 'the greatest mathematical discovery of all time'. It's easy to think he was getting a bit over-excited, but he was probably right. Compound interest is a very simple (but clever) way to make your money grow.

Suppose you put some money in the bank to save. You earn a little bit of interest. The next year, you earn some more interest on the original sum you started with – but you also earn interest on your interest. In the third year, you still earn interest on your original money. And you also earn interest on the interest you got over the last two years. Still with me?

Earning interest on your interest is the miracle of compounding. It's like throwing a stone in a still pond, and starting a little ripple which gets bigger and bigger as the circle grows. Even a little money can, over time, become a lot.

SO HOW LONG, EXACTLY?

You can work out the rough answer to that question with a method called the Rule of 72.

This is a simple sum that tells you how many years it is going to take to double your money. Take 72 and divide it by the interest rate you are getting on your savings. For example, an interest rate of 6 per cent would give $72 \div 6 = 12$. So it will take 12 years for your investment to double.

AN INSPIRATIONAL TALE

If you still don't believe me about compound interest, read your child 'The Riches of Oseola McCarthy' by Evelyn Coleman. It's a great little book.

Oseola was born in Mississippi in 1908. All of her life she worked washing other people's clothes – a backbreaking task which paid very little. In the Thirties she got just $1.50 for washing and ironing a whole bundle of clothes. And yet Oseola always saved, even though it was very little. At first it didn't amount to much, but she kept at it. Compound interest kicked in and by the end of her working life she was surprised by how much money she had amassed. She had always wanted to be a nurse but, being poorly educated, had never had the chance. Instead, she uses her money to fund places at the state university where she lives. Young people who would otherwise be unable to go to university get the education that Oseola herself missed out on.

Used like this, money is a powerful thing. Encourage your child to do the same as Oseola and one day he will be able to enjoy something which otherwise might pass him by. And he'll have done it all himself.

The saving man becomes the free man.

CHINESE PROVERB

The Pocket Money Plan

"Harris here is looking after
children's accounts"

CHAPTER FOUR

STARTING A SAVINGS ACCOUNT

The Pocket Money Plan

This chapter is here to help you teach your child about how savings and investments work. The aim, many years down the line, is that your child is able to choose what is best. I need hardly add that making good decisions in this area can make a huge difference to your life.

Once *The Pocket Money Plan* is up and running you will need a savings account. Apart from anything else, it introduces your child to the idea that there are many different people in many different places who can help with his or her money. Your child needs to be involved in the choosing process but, as this is a relationship which will last many years, you need to get it right!

BANK OR BUILDING SOCIETY?

There's very little difference between the two.

Banks are like many other large companies listed on the stock market. The directors of the business are responsible for running it

and making a profit, which is shared amongst the shareholders.

Traditionally, building societies were known as 'mutual' organisations. By opening an account you effectively became a member of the club, with a (fairly limited) say in how the club was run. As there were no shareholders to pay, the profits were shared out amongst the account holders, via the interest rates on offer.

This is why, for years, many building societies claimed that they offered higher rates of interest to their savers. However, this is no longer true. There are a few mutuals left, but many building societies have now become banks. Today's market is intensely competitive, and today there is no difference between the ability of a bank or a building society to give you a good deal – should they wish to do so.

The same applies to the savings accounts offered by large retailers and supermarkets. In fact, there may be a bank or building society behind these retailers operating their customers' accounts for them. It's always wise to find this out first. That way, you are making a more informed decision.

HOW TO EXPLAIN A SAVINGS ACCOUNT TO YOUR CHILD

Most people think the bank, building society or retailer (hereafter called the bank, for simplicity) has the upper hand. Tell your child this just isn't true. While your child should respect the bank, it only exists because of its customers, and he or she could become a very

The Pocket Money Plan

valuable one in the future.

The bank uses the money deposited by its savers to lend to other people. Those people have to pay back more than the amount they borrow, and so the bank makes a profit. It uses some of that profit to pay its savers back for the privilege of being allowed to use their money. This payment is called 'interest.'

So, having a savings account is a bit like using your money as an employee, and sending it out to work! It's a little business that works for him, day and night, rain and shine. Your child will like this idea. It makes a lot more sense than imagining his money sitting in great big piles along with everyone else's, doing nothing.

Once your child's got used to that, it gets better. If the interest payment is left in the account, the bank can use that money too – and then the interest becomes employee number two. Remember Albert Einstein and his miracle of compound interest (p89)? A savings account is where this little miracle becomes, for your child, a reality.

So that's it. You put the money in. They pay you for being able to use it while you leave it there. You take it back again, plus your payments (interest) – usually, whenever you like. It really is that simple.

HOW TO CHOOSE THE RIGHT BANK

You need to ask seven questions, preferably in this order:

1. WHERE IS IT?

Some financial experts might tell you the interest rate is the most important thing. But especially if your child is young, he needs a local bank. He is going to have a relationship with an organisation. He needs to know his money is kept in a nice, shiny building where the staff treat him, and his money, with respect.

By the time he's a teenager he may well use an internet-based account. But it's best to start off with a real place to put actual pounds and pence.

2. WHAT'S THE INTEREST RATE?

You are looking at rates for 'high street accounts'. Internet or postal account rates are available too, but not if you want a passbook that allows your child to feel connected to her money.

Sourcing the best rate can be an absolute minefield, and just scanning your high street can take an age. Instead, visit www. moneyfacts.co.uk. They do all the hard work for you, for free, by listing all the rates on offer from all the banks and building societies in the UK. To make it even easier they usually list Best Buys for each section. You're looking for the section titled

'Children's Accounts'.

There's an added bonus: the site links you to the relevant sections of the banks' sites, so you can get into the nitty gritty without the trouble of hunting down each site first.

3. ARE THERE ANY EXTRAS?

Once you've got a shortlist, look at what else is on offer. Treat any account-opening gifts and gimmicks with caution, on the basis that, if the bank didn't spend squillions on stuff you don't actually need, it could give you more in interest. But sometimes, just sometimes, the 'stuff' will be worth it.

4. WHAT'S IN THE SMALL PRINT?

In the exciting world of financial planning you will hear talk of 'headline rates'. These are interest rates designed to woo the punters and they don't often last very long. Some banks offer a rate which is far more tempting than elsewhere. Their plan is to get in a whole load of new customers and then, when they're not looking (or if they haven't read the small print) the rate becomes less competitive than the accounts which initially didn't look quite so appealing.

In general, rates on children's accounts offer much of a muchness, so be alert if you find one offering much more interest than the others. If you haven't the time or energy to move the money after six months or so, think twice before taking advantage

of the apparent generosity.

Another drawback can be the need for some kind of regular commitment to put money in. Often, to get the rate of interest advertised, your child will need to pay in a minimum monthly amount. Another wheeze is an insistence by the bank that the account always holds a minimum balance.

In my experience the simplest, most straightforward savings accounts, devoid of bells and whistles, and easy to understand, are usually the best option.

5. HOW WILL THINGS CHANGE AS YOUR CHILD GETS OLDER?

The bank usually sets the terms for its children's savings accounts according to age. Part of this is a practical thing. By law, children under seven can only hold an account with an adult – so that person will always be required to authorise any withdrawals. Above seven, your child can hold an account on his or her own. But until your child reaches 12 it remains very straightforward, operated by a passbook which records the amount saved.

Most accounts, give your child increasing access as he gets older, culminating in a cash card which allows him to make as many withdrawals as he likes. Now we hope that instilling Pocket Money Plan principles from a young age means that, when temptation knocks, your child will be money savvy enough to pay no heed. However, giving him a cash card and access to an account containing money is a fairly big deal. So think carefully, and make sure you know what the deal is in your child's case.

6. WHAT'S THEIR LITERATURE LIKE?

Again, some financial experts might say that this doesn't matter. But my question is this: does the bank address you, or the young person doing it the honour of becoming its customer? We need as much help as we can get to teach out children about money. The least you can expect is that the bank will help by writing to your child now again – and, you hope, provide some guidance on money matters.

7. ASK AROUND

You may have friends with older children who have already chosen a savings account. Ask why they chose that bank, and how it has performed since.

If you have a financial adviser, especially one who is independent, ask them for an opinion too. Most will be glad to give a good customer a few minutes free of charge. Naturally they'll go to www.moneyfacts.co.uk, just as you can do – but they will also know which Best Buys tend to stay competitive in the long term. That in turn shows which banks tend to take children more seriously.

ONCE YOU'RE UP AND RUNNING

From time to time, check the interest your child is receiving against what's available elsewhere. But don't be too hasty. Moving involves paperwork and time. Only if the bank really doesn't seem to be delivering rate-wise should you take your child's cash to a competitor who appreciates the business a bit more.

TO OPEN THE ACCOUNT

As with most things in life there's a form to fill in. The bank also has to check you are who you say you are, and that you live where you say you do. Generally, a driving licence or passport, plus a utility bill or bank statement, will be enough. If your child is over seven, he'll be included in the check too. Ring to check first. And please be patient: it's the law.

TAX FOR KIDS
SAD BUT TRUE

The tax man is not known for his generosity and it is by no means guaranteed that your child will escape his evil claws.
The good news is that your child has a personal tax

allowance, just as a grown-up does. So he or she can earn up to the basic tax rate each year without paying income tax. With savings, it's not quite so straightforward. There's no limit to the amount you can invest for a child but, if the resulting interest is £100 or more, it will be taxed as if you had earned the money, not them. Sneaky! If you are a two-parent family children get to earn £100 for each parent, doubling the allowance. But it's still harsh. (On savings money a child's earned he or she can get away without paying tax on the interest. Just fill in Inland Revenue Form R85.)

HOWEVER...

Grandparents, friends and other relatives can give as much money as they like without interest being taxed as their income. If gifts like this are a regular occurrence in your family, you may need to keep yourself (and your child) on the straight and narrow. The best way is to open a separate account for these funds, so that the money given by you, and the money given by them, can be clearly identified.

THE £100 RULE

The taxman has put measures in place to ensure that parents don't save their own money in their children's accounts. By doing this (assuming the children had no real savings of their own), parents

could earn tax-free interest up to the basic rate of tax, instead of paying tax at their normal rate.

That's where the £100 rule comes in. Basically, if you put enough money in your child's savings account to earn him more than £100 in interest in a year, the tax man assumes that it's your money, not his, and levies tax at the rate you pay. This is regardless of whether the money genuinely belongs to your child or not. Nasty.

HERE'S AN EXAMPLE.

Lucky Lucy, aged nine, has £8,000 in her building society account. Dad has contributed £3,000, mum £1,000 and her generous aunt Jenny has coughed up £4,000. As the money given by Dad generates more than £100 of interest in a year, Lucy can't avoid having tax taken off.

The example below shows exactly how this works. Just in case you're not sure 'gross' means 'without tax taken off' and 'net' means 'after tax' – just like on a pay slip.

Dad's contribution

- Dad's £3,000 produced gross interest of **£150**
- The amount the building society took off for tax was **£30**
- The 'net' interest is **£120**

Normally, if a child earns less interest on a savings account than the basic rate tax allowance he or she can complete tax form R85 and claim back from the Inland Revenue any money that the bank or building society had deducted (often this form is completed when the account is opened).

The problem here is that the tax man assumes Lucy's dad is sheltering his own money in her account – even though he is just a lovely, generous man. Her interest is treated as part of his earned income, and taxed accordingly.

Mum's contribution

- Mum's £1,000 produced gross interest of **£50**
- The amount the building society took off for tax was **£10**
- The 'net' interest is **£40**

As the gross interest is under £100, Lucy's parents can claim back for her the £10 that was taken off using Form R85.

Generous Jenny's contribution

- Her £4,000 produced gross interest of **£200**
- The amount the building society took off for tax was **£40**
- The 'net' interest is **£160**

As the £100 rule applies only to parents, Lucy can also claim back this £40.

So, at some point, your child's savings could grow to the point where he or she can make their money work harder by moving some of it elsewhere. It's called 'diversifying', and it's the subject of the next chapter.

An investment in knowledge always pays the best interest.

BENJAMIN FRANKLIN

The Pocket Money Plan

"If you have to invest money to make
money, how do you get *started*?"

CHAPTER
FIVE

INVESTING

The Pocket Money Plan

Investing is the next step up from a savings account. It's what you do when you want to make some of your money work harder for you than it can in the bank or building society.

Even thinking about investments might feel a long way from where you are at the moment, but I promise that if your child (or indeed you) manages to save regularly there will come a time when it will feel right.

Of course the world of investing has a reputation for being scary, impenetrable and confusing. It's something 'other people' do, people who 'understand these things'. It's certainly true that not many people, young or old, feel confident around investments. But, as I intend to show you, they are remarkably simple. There are only five ways you can invest directly in something, and I'll explain each of them in turn. There's also a sixth form of investment, which is indirect – in other words, you pay a professional to do it for you.

In every case the idea is the same: plant your money 'seeds' in the right place, wait patiently, and voila! – you should have more than you'd ever have got by leaving it in your savings account.

WHY DO I NEED TO LEARN ABOUT INVESTING FOR MY CHILD?

Investing is the hardest money subject to grasp, but what if I said it is a way of preparing for your child's university fees while he's still in nappies? You should invest (if and when you have the spare cash) because it makes life easier. There are so many expensive events ahead. A first car? That gap year? A deposit on a house? A wedding? Ask yourself how well-placed you or your child will be to pay for them when the time comes.

So it makes sense to use every resource available to you to help your child's money (and your own) to grow. Without the multiplying power of an investment, paying for these things might be difficult or even impossible. So think of the knowledge in this chapter as a helping hand.

And, as this is *The Pocket Money Plan*, you won't be surprised if I point out that the investment experience is hugely valuable for your child. Making money grow in this way takes a certain level of knowledge and skill – just as driving a car does, or passing an exam. The great thing about investing, however, is that you and your child can choose exactly how difficult you want it to be. And once a child learns the principles, he or she will be equipped with what could turn out to be a crucial ability in later life.

IT'S NOT YOU, IT'S THEM!

There are enough financial products out there to daunt the strongest heart. Although at first glance they look confusing, I am going to show you that they're not. Some investment professionals (and politicians for that matter) might want you to think otherwise, but that's only because it makes them feel important.

The number one turn-off is the habit investment people have of using lots of stupid words. Words in the wrong context, words with different meanings, acronyms no-one in their right mind could ever guess. Just knowing this simple fact – that it's not you, it's them – is a nugget of gold.

I've explained all of these words and terms at the back of the book, starting on page 216, but I'll also explain them here as we go along. Let me give you a couple of examples. First, the words 'short', 'medium', 'long', and 'term'. Ordinary words, but in investment language they have particular meanings.

'Short term' is any period less than 5 years.

'Medium term' is 5-10 years.

'Long term' is more than 10 years.

Here's another example: 'interest', 'growth', 'gain, and 'return'.

When we talk about savings the money we make is called 'interest'.

When we talk about investments the money we make is called 'growth' or 'returns'.

When we talk about savings or investments the money we

make is a 'gain'.

There is hardly any difference in meaning between the four words, and you can use them interchangeably.

HOW TO MAKE INVESTING EXCITING FOR YOUR CHILD

If a savings account is a way of getting your money to work for you, then investing is the same thing on steroids. Depending on which investment we choose, we can have the directors of massive companies working for us, both here and abroad. Brilliant statisticians and investment managers all over the world could be toiling for us, even when we are asleep, looking after our interests. People in all walks of life, from architects and engineers to cleaners and caretakers, will be doing their bit in shiny skyscrapers, vast factories or huge shopping centres, tiny bits of which could be owned by you or your children. Our money could be drilling for oil or digging for gold. It might even be lent to the Government, in which case they'll have to pay us for the pleasure!

This is exactly what happens when you and your child invest money. It was tough finding the money to save in the first place. Now it's payback time. Let's find some people to work for us. Let's find thousands of people, all over the world.

THE MONEY MOUNTAIN

One way of seeing investments in relation to a savings
account is the Money Mountain.

ARE WE READY TO INVEST?

For the purposes of teaching your child about money, saving is
the habit of laying some regular money aside, and if he puts it in
a savings account it accumulates a little more quickly. An added
bonus is that if life doesn't go to plan, or it's being saved for short-
term goals, the money is usually easy to withdraw.

Investing takes things a stage further, by allowing your child
(and his or her money) to take on a bit more responsibility. In
return, it should work even harder, and start to build into a Money
Mountain. It's not quite as accessible as before, so investing is only
a medium and long term thing.

So, how much money you should you have saved in an account
before you think about investing?

The answer, unsurprisingly, is that it depends. We all have different family situations, different aspirations and different attitudes. But the most important factor is your goal: just what is it that you want to do for your child (or that your child wants to do for him or herself) that involves money in five, ten or more years? University fees? A place to live? A decent set of wheels? Whatever it might be, just as with saving, you investment goal needs to be SMART. If it passes that test, and if it's several years off, it makes a lot of sense to consider investing.

Here are a few other 'critical moments' that can suggest it's time for your child to invest some money:

● When the £100 rule means that interest on the money you give your child will be taxed.

● When your child's savings account has more money in it than is likely to be needed in the next ten years.

● When half the money in his savings account is enough for an investment product that looks good.

● When your child is ready to learn more about money.

THE THREE GOLDEN RULES OF INVESTING

1. SPLIT YOUR MONEY UP

Called 'diversifying' in financial jargon, the technique of splitting your savings and investment money into different 'pots' makes good sense. At least one of those pots should always be an ordinary savings account, to give your Money Mountain a firm foundation. On top will be one or more investments. Together, your collection of pots is known as an 'investment portfolio'. Trying various different things in a portfolio (diversifying, if you prefer) is crucial because, with investing, we will not always be successful. It's a case of not putting all your eggs in one basket – or, if you prefer, of having a finger in several different pies. If one pie proves too hot to handle then at least the fingers in the other pies won't get too burnt.

2. UNDERSTAND THE RISK

I must be the harbinger of doom and tell you that, whilst investing can achieve great things, the returns are not guaranteed. You may even get back less than you invested. In other words, there is a risk involved. Nothing in life is ever straightforward and if we didn't know this before we had children, I'm sure we all know it now.

So the value of an investment can go up and down. This fluctuation is called 'volatility'. Usually, the higher the risk involved with an investment, the higher the volatility. But, at the same time, the greater the potential return.

The foundation of your child's Money Mountain, the savings account, will always be almost entirely safe. But to build on that foundation involves a certain amount of risk. You need to understand how much risk comes with any particular investment (more on this later), and compare it with how much risk you are willing to take.

THE RISK SLOPE

Different investments involve different levels of risk. Just as on a real mountain, only you can decide how far up the slope you are willing to travel – and how far you are willing to let your child go. Without that conscious decision you are in the investment wilderness.

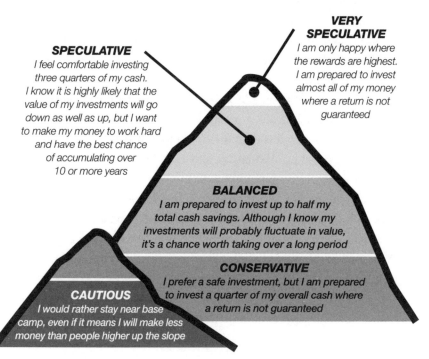

VERY SPECULATIVE
I am only happy where the rewards are highest. I am prepared to invest almost all of my money where a return is not guaranteed

SPECULATIVE
I feel comfortable investing three quarters of my cash. I know it is highly likely that the value of my investments will go down as well as up, but I want to make my money to work hard and have the best chance of accumulating over 10 or more years

BALANCED
I am prepared to invest up to half my total cash savings. Although I know my investments will probably fluctuate in value, it's a chance worth taking over a long period

CONSERVATIVE
I prefer a safe investment, but I am prepared to invest a quarter of my overall cash where a return is not guaranteed

CAUTIOUS
I would rather stay near base camp, even if it means I will make less money than people higher up the slope

Are you beginning to work out where you might sit on the slope?

3. GET YOUR TIME FRAME RIGHT

Of all the wonderful things your child has on his or her side, the most precious is time. You may be wiser, richer, more accomplished in a thousand ways – but the truth is you almost certainly have less time than your child does. And where risk is concerned, that makes a big difference. Here's why.

So far it's clear that, because the value of an investment can go up and down (fluctuate), you might not get back the amount that you invested. But wait. If you have time, you can afford to look at things differently.

Suppose you invest on a Monday. The ink has hardly dried on the deal when risk strikes a mortal blow – and by Tuesday your investment is worth less than the day before. If you need to reach your savings goal on Wednesday, and 'cash in' your investment, you've lost out.

With children, you can afford not to be so short-termist. Let's say you are incredibly well organised, and you have decided to fund your child's university costs while he or she is still in nappies. With 18 years to wait, you can afford to stand tall in the battle with risk. If you invest one year, and your investment goes down the next, you still have 16 years left during which the money can recover.

As a rule, the longer the time period, the more likely it is that the days when you lose money will be outweighed by the days you make money.

Now look at the risk slope again – and ask yourself whether, marching slowly with time on your hands, you may just want to wander a little nearer to the summit than you thought.

WHAT TO INVEST IN?

Here we go, you're thinking. There must be at least a million things to invest in. I'm about to lose the will to live in a rat's nest of obscure terms, pointless complication and financial befuddlement.

Wrong. Remember: it's not you, it's them. Here in the UK, we invest in just five things:

● Cash
● Gilts and bonds
● Property
● Shares
● Commodities

Everything you see described as an investment will be a variation on one of these themes – and what your money buys is almost certainly either one of these things, or a mixture.

You can invest in two ways:
● Directly – by buying one of the five things above;
● Indirectly – by buying a package of investments bundled together as an 'investment product'.

Understanding the difference between a direct investment and an indirect investment/investment product is the key to realising how this stuff works. The vast majority of people reading this will go for indirect – at least to start with – but as this approach is itself made up of direct investments you need to know the lowdown on them first. Fortunately, that's pretty straightforward. Think of them as items you buy without any packaging.

As we go through the options you might think some of the sums involved are a bit ambitious for your child, but bear with me. It will all make sense in the end.

DIRECT INVESTMENTS

1. CASH

As you know, cash works for you if you allow it to build up in a savings account. The payment (known as interest) is a firm foundation of any Money Mountain because the returns are virtually guaranteed.

The only potential risk is that the interest you receive (remembering that you might have to pay some tax) needs to keep ahead of inflation. If it doesn't, then the real value of your money decreases. If inflation is 2.5 per cent per year, and the interest you receive is only two per cent, then after a year your money will be worth half a per cent less.

 Low Risk
Works for the short,
medium or long term
Your money is easily
accessible.

 *There's the chance
of greater rewards
elsewhere.
Inflation can dent
the return on your
investment.
You might have to pay
tax on your interest*

Good if
✔ *You classify
yourself as cautious.*
✔ *You might need
access to your
money quickly.*
✔ *The time period
of investment is
short.*

WHO DECIDES THE INTEREST RATES

Interest is the amount which a bank, building society,
company or even Government will pay you for the
privilege of using your money. Banks and building
societies use your money to lend it to others. Companies
use it to fund new projects, or to expand their operations.
Governments use it to help run the country.

The interest rate you get in return for lending these
people your money is tied to the 'base rate', set by the Bank
of England. Your rate will be termed 'above base' or 'below

base', depending on where the Bank of England's base
rate is at that moment.

The Bank does this to control inflation. When goods and
services get more expensive, inflation rises. This devalues
everybody's money, because the same amount will then buy
fewer goods and services. To keep the economy stable,
and ensure that money retains its value, the Bank tries to
control the 'price' of money.

So, the base rate affects not just your savings account, but also
on money you lend to companies (known as Corporate Bonds)
and money you lend to the Government (known as Gilts).

2. GILTS AND BONDS

Also known as Fixed Risk Securities, Gilts and Bonds lie a little
further up the slope on the Money Mountain.

The words may be unfamiliar, but the meaning is simple. They're
just another way that you can lend your money to someone and
get him or her to pay you for the privilege. If you lend your money
to a company, a Bond or 'Corporate Bond' is a promise to pay you
in return. If you lend your money to the Government, the promise
to repay is a 'Gilt-Edged Security' – Gilts for short. In both cases,
the agreed date for repayment is called the 'redemption date'.

All the time the company or Government is using your money,

you receive a fixed sum of interest at regular intervals. But often, instead of being called interest, it is referred to as the 'bond yield'. Generally, this yield is better than you would get in a savings account. Of course, with that better return comes a risk: although you will continue to get your interest, the value of the Bond (ie the amount you lent in the first place) can go up and down. So you may not get back all of the money you invested.

If you need the money invested in a bond before the redemption date, you can sell the bond on the open market at any time. The price will be the market price of the bond at the time you sell – which could be more or less than you would get if you wait until the redemption date.

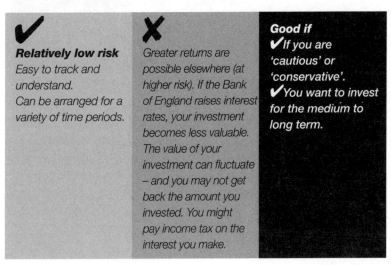

✔

Relatively low risk
Easy to track and understand.
Can be arranged for a variety of time periods.

✗

Greater returns are possible elsewhere (at higher risk). If the Bank of England raises interest rates, your investment becomes less valuable. The value of your investment can fluctuate – and you may not get back the amount you invested. You might pay income tax on the interest you make.

Good if
✔*If you are 'cautious' or 'conservative'.*
✔*You want to invest for the medium to long term.*

3. PROPERTY

Hugely fashionable in recent years. Buying property is dead simple – in theory, anyway. You buy a house in the belief that someone will be willing to pay more for it at some time in the future. If they do, you've made a profit.

In the meantime you may be able to rent the building out, and

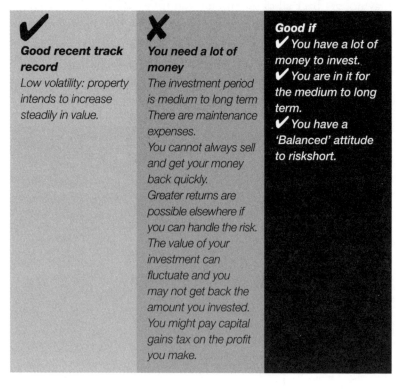

Good recent track record

Low volatility: property intends to increase steadily in value.

You need a lot of money

The investment period is medium to long term

There are maintenance expenses.

You cannot always sell and get your money back quickly.

Greater returns are possible elsewhere if you can handle the risk.

The value of your investment can fluctuate and you may not get back the amount you invested.

You might pay capital gains tax on the profit you make.

Good if
✔ You have a lot of money to invest.
✔ You are in it for the medium to long term.
✔ You have a 'Balanced' attitude to riskshort.

gain an income this way too. Residential buildings are rented to ordinary people, while commercial property is rented to a company or organisation.

The risks are fairly straightforward. The property may not increase in value. Maintaining any building costs cash, and this can be more than expected. The tenants might become unable to pay the rent, or it may be difficult to find a tenant in the first place.

On top of all that, property is relatively hard to get rid of. There is always a risk that no-one wants to buy at all, or that they are not willing to pay what you think it is worth.

4. SHARES

Shares (also known as stocks, stakes and equities) are where you can really push the boat out in terms of getting a worldwide staff of thousands on your books. Companies all over the globe put themselves up for sale to willing 'shareholders'.

And, for once, this is an investment that means exactly what it says: a share. As a shareholder you own the proportion of the company you have invested in. Admittedly, this is usually extremely small, but you (or your child) owns a bit of it just the same.

In return for buying your 'bit' of the company you are entitled to a share in the value of what the company is worth. If the value of the company rises, you have achieved 'growth' on your share (you may have to pay Capital Gains Tax on your gain when you come to sell). You also receive a share of the company's profits at regular intervals, called a 'dividend' or 'yield'. Again, you may have to pay tax on dividends.

The risks are quite simple: the company's value may fall or stay the same – in which case the value of your shares will do likewise. If the company becomes completely unloved, it could be that no one wants to buy your share when you want to sell. Worse still, the company could go bust – in which case you could lose out completely. And of course, if profits are poor or non-existent, you may get less of a dividend – or even none at all.

✔	✘	Good if
Good potential rewards. Easy to spread the risk across several companies. Your investment value is easy to track.	High potential risk. Best suited to medium or long term. You need to keep a close eye on how your investment is doing. You might pay tax on your profits.	✔ You can afford a long investment period. ✔ You don't mind taking a bit of risk. ✔ You are interested in 'your' companies.

A QUICK GUIDE TO SHARES

People are always buying and selling shares via the 'stock market'. To learn more about how it works, visit www. londonstockexchange.co.uk.

The price of shares depends on many factors, and can fluctuate on an almost daily basis. Professional buyers on the stock exchange assess how successful a company will be, and the share price reflects their conclusions. They will consider a company's current value, and study its plans for the future (and therefore potential profits). Sometimes they look at the current staff and decide whether a change in management is afoot that could change the company's fortunes.

Picking the best shares to buy can be tricky, but you can get help from a 'stockbroker' – someone who researches what the values of companies are likely to be in the future, and hence can suggest whether or not you should buy them. They will normally charge you for this advice.

If the company you are investing in makes any money, you are entitled to a share of the profits once a year, called a dividend. You can choose to have your dividend paid to you immediately, or you can use the cash to invest in more of the company's shares. You'd take the money if you were investing to create a regular income (not that usual with children), though you might have to pay tax on it. Re-investing makes more sense if you're trying to make your money grow for the future.

When you sell your shares ('encash' them, in investment language) you effectively sell them to someone else via the stock market. Choosing the best time to sell can be nerve racking!

HAVE FUN WITH SHARES – FOR FREE!

Your child can have lots of fun investing in shares, even if you've no money!

Suppose your child supports a big football team. Why not create a fantasy share portfolio? It's easy to track the club's share price online or in the newspapers, and see whether it goes up or down. Children can take this a step further by seeing how the team performs against another in the same league. What effect does performance on the pitch have on the share price?

There are plenty of other options besides football. How about a favourite band signed to a particular record label? Or the film company behind the latest film your child's seen? Or the label on trainers? Next time he comes home with yet another pair completely obliterated, you can show exactly how much money a new pair is making for the shareholders.

If you have two children close in age, things can get competitive. You could put up a cash prize for the winner after a few months, perhaps put aside to enable them to buy some shares for real.

5. COMMODITIES

These are nothing more than the raw materials used to make the things we buy. They could occur naturally (oil, gas, gold, diamonds, metals), or grow in farms and forests (wood, wheat, sugar, coffee, cows, pigs).

Commodity prices rise and fall according to demand. If you buy ten barrels of oil and the price of oil goes up, you've made a gain. If the world's wheat producers have a bumper year, the price might fall – in which case, you hope you haven't bought any wheat!

As you can see, this is a form of investing that suits very experienced people. It is quite rare for individuals to invest directly in commodities, and those who do normally employ a 'commodities broker' to help (and pay a fee for the service).

Sometimes, investors don't actually buy the commodity itself, but instead take a bet on whether the price will rise and fall. This can get extremely risky.

Commodities can sometimes be a good idea if other kinds of investment aren't performing well, for example if the stock market is under-performing.

5. Commodities

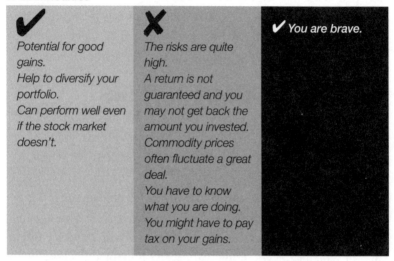

✔	✘	✔ You are brave.
Potential for good gains. Help to diversify your portfolio. Can perform well even if the stock market doesn't.	The risks are quite high. A return is not guaranteed and you may not get back the amount you invested. Commodity prices often fluctuate a great deal. You have to know what you are doing. You might have to pay tax on your gains.	

ARE DIRECT INVESTMENTS FOR ME OR MY CHILD?

Now you know about the five 'homes' for your money when you invest directly, you can make a decision. All five categories (often known as 'asset classes') are relatively easy to understand and, most importantly, it's clear where most of them stand on the Risk Slope.

The benefit of having five classes of asset is that you can have a

real mixture in your portfolio. With all of your fingers in different pies, the overall risk reduces. And, of course, there is room to diversify within each of the assets themselves. We can use more than one bank for a savings account, pick different kinds of property, buy bonds in almost any type of company, and so on. Shares are particularly suited to diversifying, and if you buy them directly you really should spread the risk by choosing different companies and industries.

But having said all that, most people don't have the confidence or time to invest in this way. The margin for error in choosing 'which gilt?' or 'which share?' feels too great. And property is a non-starter for most because of the sheer amount of money involved.

But that need not be the end of investing for you. We still have Indirect Investments. And if, having considered Direct Investments, you don't fancy getting involved, then trust me: these are much more likely to be your cup of tea.

INDIRECT INVESTMENTS

So far we've looked at the five classes of investment: cash, gilts or bonds, property, shares or commodities. And you understand that a good mix of all five is the best overall approach. Nevertheless, it's quite possible that you've decided that none of them suits you at the moment.

Fortunately, there is another way to get the benefits of investing, without the hassle: get an expert to make the decisions for you (phew!).

Investment managers (also known as fund managers) are gorgeous people, because they take the direct investments and package them into 'boxes' to suit all tastes and budgets. These 'boxes' are known as 'investment products'. Obviously they're not real boxes, but the bundling together of different investments is real enough. And it's a good idea, because it means you sub-contract the choice of investments to a being of superior knowledge.

WHY A 'BOX' OF INVESTMENTS MAKES SENSE

Gilts, shares, property and the rest offer investors a 'take it or leave it' scenario. But indirect investments allow you to choose the 'box' that's best for you. It's easy to pick a box too, because all of them conform to six simple rules which tell you:

1. Who is eligible to 'buy' or invest in the box
2. What kinds of investments can and cannot be put inside the box
3. If there is a minimum or maximum amount you can invest
4. When and if you can be paid an income from the box
5. How any profits you make will be taxed
6. When you can sell the box and get your money back

Suddenly, even if you struggle with the concept of investing, you can have a good idea of what is likely to happen to your money, and which product feels right.

BUT IT GETS BETTER

As well as deciding which investments go inside your box, the investment manager has his or her own box. This box is absolutely colossal. Inside are many different kinds of direct investments worth many millions of pounds. This 'super box' is called a 'fund'. I've you've heard of investment funds, it's the same thing.

When you buy an investment product (your smaller box), the investment manager doesn't just give you one or two random investments from the bigger box. Instead you get a tiny share of every single investment in the fund. This tiny share is called a 'unit'.

The brilliance of this is that, for the money it would have cost you to make one or two direct investments, you've bought into hundreds. And the reason that's possible is because the investment manager has pooled your money with everyone else's. It's like having a little help from your friends, on the basis that friends are only people we haven't met yet. And it means that, even if you only have a small amount of money to invest, you can spread the risk across a wide range of investments.

So instead of having a couple of fingers in a couple of pies, you club together with other people to put hundreds of fingers in hundreds of pies.

HOW FUNDS ARE TAILORED TO SUIT YOU

Each manager's fund contains a combination of investments designed to achieve a particular 'investment strategy'. That strategy is the game plan the investment manager has for making your money mountain grow.

The investment product you 'buy' might have room for just one 'strategy' – or, by giving you a slice of various different funds, it might have several. This is yet another way in which the box can spread your risk.

So what are these strategies? The most important is risk. Each fund is rated for risk, depending on how far up the slope the fund manager decides to go. The time period is also crucial.

The fund might focus on one kind of direct investment – for example corporate bonds. Or it might target a particular industrial sector, such as pharmaceuticals or telecommunications. Or the strategy might centre on direct investments in one country or geographical area, so you could choose a North American Fund or an Asian Fund. These kinds of funds obviously choose a mix of different investments, so, it won't just be, for example, US company shares, but perhaps also some US gilts. There is normally always a little cash.

In mixing these ingredients in different ways the investment manager aims for the return he or she is looking for, bearing in mind the risk he or she has decided to take. A cautious fund might have more money invested in cash, gilts and property, while a riskier one would give more weight to company shares. This process is called 'asset allocation'.

WHERE'S THE CATCH?

An Investment Manager is a highly qualified and knowledgeable person, often with teams of analysts running around after him or her. So you are going to have to pay him handsomely to choose what should and should not go into the box.

Normally, this is a price well worth paying. If you go for direct investments, you can often rack up expensive administration costs such as buying and selling, collecting dividends and income, and dealing with foreign stock exchanges and brokers. By joining with others and investing indirectly you are effectively buying in bulk, and there are discounts to be had. And the more of your money you don't spend on costs, the more chance of making a profit.

So there's usually no catch, beyond choosing the best indirect investment for you. And that's the subject of the next chapter.

An investor without investment objectives is like a traveller without a destination.

RALPH SEGER

"...and I'm pleased to report that your stock
portfolio has matured well beyond yourself, Max."

CHAPTER
SIX

INVESTMENT
SERVICES

INVESTMENT FUNDS FOR CHILDREN

The main ones you need to know about are:

- **Child trust Funds**
- **Friendly society investments**
- **National savings**
- **Unit trusts**
- **Investment trusts**
- **Stakeholder pensions**

Each of these products has different objectives, styles of working and tax implications, and in theory the ideal child's portfolio would contain them all. In practice that's unlikely, so it helps to know how each of them works so that you can choose the one or two that suit you best.

The system for choosing is simple and, I hope by now, familiar. It's based on your:

- **Savings objective**
- **Attitude to risk**
- **Time available**

CHILD TRUST FUND

If you have a young child, or are planning to, you definitely need to concentrate. This is stuff you need to know.

The government are keen that we teach our children about money, that we talk to them about it and that they grow up with a financial cushion, no matter how small. The Child Trust Fund, or CTF, is their way offering to help. And, for once, I think they've done a good job.

A CTF is an investment product, which means it's a 'Box' we can put different kinds of direct and indirect investments into. The Rules of the Box (p128) tell us more about how it works.

CHILD TRUST FUND RULES

● **Who is eligible?**

All children born on or after 1 September 2002 who live in the UK and are eligible for Child Benefit. Anyone can contribute: you, your wider family, friends – even children.

● **What kind of investment can go inside the Box?**

There are three types of CTF to choose from:

1. CTF SAVINGS ACCOUNTS

Here, the investment inside the Box is straightforward cash.

This kind of CTF is just like a normal savings account, but with some special rules.

2. STAKEHOLDER CTF ACCOUNTS

These are available from many insurance companies, investment companies and Friendly Societies. The investments inside the Box are indirect, so an investment manager decides them. You buy units in the manager's fund, so this is an example of a 'pooled' investment.

Most CTF Funds keep it simple and try to mirror the growth in the stock market. This kind of Fund is known as a FTSE Tracker (pronounced 'Footsie', and standing for Financial Times and London Stock Exchange). So the value of this investment can fluctuate and returns are not guaranteed. There is some risk involved.

If you invest in a Stakeholder CTF, the Fund Manager has to start moving the money into lower-risk investments when your child is 13. By 18, it must all be in cash.

3. SHARES ACCOUNT CTF

These allow you to buy shares as Direct Investments.

Which of the three you choose depends on the amount of risk you want to take. If you are cautious or conservative you may go for the savings option where the returns are stable and virtually guaranteed. But remember time is on your side. You have 18 years to invest, and a long period can help to reduce the risk. The Barclays Capital Equity Gilt Study showed that shares outperformed savings accounts for all but one 18-year period between 1889 and 2006.

3. IS THERE IS A MINIMUM OR MAXIMUM AMOUNT YOU CAN INVEST?

The only rule is that you can invest no more than £1,200 a year. The government helps out by giving £250 when your child is born, and more (possibly another £250) when he or she reaches seven. You receive a voucher automatically when you make a claim for Child Benefit, and take it to the bank, building society or investment company.

WHAT IS A CHILD TRUST FUND WORTH?

Take the plunge by investing more than the Government's £250 voucher, and you'll see a big difference in your child's Money Mountain by the time he or she's 18.

Monthly contribution	Potential amount by age 18
£0	**£1,000**
£10	**£4,700**
£20	**£8,300**

continued over page

continued from previous page

Monthly contribution	Potential amount by age 18
£30	**£11,900**
£40	**£15,500**
£50	**£19,100**
£60	**£22,700**
£70	**£26,300**
£80	**£29,900**
£90	**£33,500**
£100	**£37,100**

These projections are based on money invested for 18 years in a stakeholder Child Trust Fund account, alongside the government's initial £250 and another £250 at age seven, with yearly growth at the FSA mid-rate of seven per cent. The figures are not guaranteed: remember shares can go down as well as up.

Source: Children's Mutual

HOW YOU CAN ACCESS YOUR MONEY?

The money is locked away until your child is 18, at which point it will be legally his or hers. Some people worry about this, but

if you've brought your child up with *The Pocket Money Plan* it shouldn't be an issue.

WHEN WILL INCOME BE PAID?

As all of the money is locked away, any interest or income stays inside the Box.

HOW WILL PROFITS BE TAXED?

It won't – which is one of the major benefits of a CTF. And for parents, the £100 rule doesn't apply.

And here's a little tax tip: if friends and grandparents want to help save for your child, and you can afford to put the maximum £1200 a year into the CTF, ask them to invest elsewhere. This is because they are unaffected by the £100 rule, while the CTF is the one place where you can avoid it!

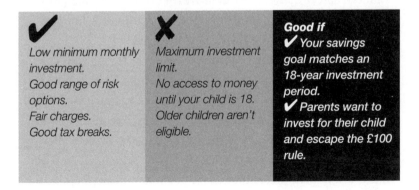

✔	✗	Good if
Low minimum monthly investment.	Maximum investment limit.	✔ Your savings goal matches an 18-year investment period.
Good range of risk options.	No access to money until your child is 18.	✔ Parents want to invest for their child and escape the £100 rule.
Fair charges.	Older children aren't eligible.	
Good tax breaks.		

CHILD TRUST FUND BASICS

Government rules say that no CTF account can have charges of more than 1.5 per cent a year, and the minimum contribution is just £10.

Each child can only have one CTF account, but you can switch between a Savings account, Stakeholder account or Share CTF provider at any time. But remember this takes time and effort, and also a charge for Stakeholders and Shares.

If you don't open a CTF account within 12 months of receiving the voucher, HM Revenue & Customs will automatically open a stakeholder CTF for you. The company they choose will be random and although you can move the account for free (when you get round to it), it's always best to organise this yourself before HMRC gets involved.

Some sections of the community have very strong views on where their money is invested. Shari'a accounts, for example, are based on Islamic values, and do not invest in areas such as alcohol, tobacco and gambling. Many people also want to consider ethical investing. If this applies to you there are various providers offering a solution that allows you to stick with your principles. Find out more at www.childtrustfund.co.uk and www.moneyfacts.co.uk.

UNIT TRUSTS

A Unit Trust is basically a Box into which we put direct investments chosen by a Fund Manager. It can provide lots of flexibility and is certainly worth considering for you and your child if you are willing to move a little up the Risk Slope. To all intents and purposes it's the same as something you may come across called an OEIC (Open Ended Investment Company).

WHO IS ELIGIBLE TO BUY OR INVEST IN THE BOX?

Although your child has to be 18 to have a Unit Trust, you can still invest in one with the intention of handing the money over later. Your child can provide some or all of the cash too. The legal owner (for now) of the investment is you, but it can be 'designated' for your child, and will in that case belong to him or her at 18. You will need a bit of paperwork in place (called a Bare Trust).

WHAT KINDS OF INVESTMENT CAN BE PUT INSIDE THE BOX?

This is where Unit Trusts become interesting because the world is your oyster. Essentially, the Fund Manager decides what direct investments to put inside his or her 'Box' or Fund, and you buy 'units' of this Fund to put inside your own 'Box' (in this case, the Unit Trust).

There are many Funds to choose from, and the enormous spread of their individual investments gives you the maximum opportunity to spread your risk by diversifying. Most Unit Trusts house units from two or more different Funds, and because these Funds range anywhere between 'cautious' and 'highly speculative' you can choose investments which very closely match your risk profile.

Fund Managers sometimes employ a strategy of investing only in property – something most people can't afford to do on their own. You might be Funding a share in a shopping centre near you, a landmark office building or some des res you could normally never afford! Getting into property in this way allows you to diversify without going too far up the risk scale.

IS THERE A MINIMUM OF MAXIMUM AMOUNT YOU CAN INVEST?

The minimum can be as low as £500 for a one-off investment, or £25 a month, although most Unit Trusts stipulate a minimum £50 a month. You can start and stop monthly contributions whenever you want. There is no maximum.

HOW DO YOU ACCESS YOUR MONEY?

Unit Trusts have no fixed timescale for investment. You buy or sell units through the Fund Manager whenever you like, although because of the risk involved you would normally only consider the medium or long term. The value of the units in your 'Box' changes in line with the overall value of the investments in the Fund Manager's bigger 'Box'. Over time you hope that means it will rise, but values can fluctuate, returns are not guaranteed and you may not get back all of the money that you invested.

You can set up a Unit Trust to generate growth, instead of income. The bad news is, you have to pay Capital Gains Tax (CGT) on the growth. The good news is, everyone, including your child, is entitled to a CGT allowance – that's an amount of money you can make in any tax year without paying any CGT.

HOW UNIT TRUST HELPS WITH UNIVERSITY FEES

The great thing about Unit Trusts is their flexibility – you can sell the units gradually. Here's an example:
Mr Smith invests £5,000 for his daughter Ann, aged 8 in 2007.

In 2017 she will be 18, and ready for university.
While she is still young he can afford to choose fairly high
risk Funds for his Unit Trust. But as she approaches school
leaving age he switches to lower risk investments – perhaps
even a cash Fund. He doesn't want to risk a Fund dipping in
value just when he needs the money.

He draws out the money in stages, to suit Ann's needs: a
third in her first year of study, another third in her second year
and the final third in her last year. In this way he also reduces his
potential tax liability, because he is 'realising' his gain over three
tax years instead of one.

CAN INCOME BE PAID?

The investments inside a Unit Trust Box will generate interest
or dividends. As with shares, you can choose to take the money
as regular income, or reinvest it to buy more units.

HOW WILL PROFITS BE TAXED?

The gain you make on the Growth of your investment is
potentially liable for Capital Gains Tax.

As for the interest and dividends, the fund manager pays some
tax from inside the Fund. You shouldn't have any more tax to pay
unless adding the money to your other income makes you
a higher rate tax payer.

Unit Trusts

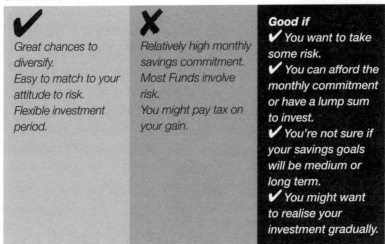

✔	✖	**Good if**
Great chances to diversify.	Relatively high monthly savings commitment.	✔ You want to take some risk.
Easy to match to your attitude to risk.	Most Funds involve risk.	✔ You can afford the monthly commitment or have a lump sum to invest.
Flexible investment period.	You might pay tax on your gain.	✔ You're not sure if your savings goals will be medium or long term.
		✔ You might want to realise your investment gradually.

INVESTMENT TRUSTS

In many ways, these are very similar to Unit Trusts, with an investment manager choosing a range of direct investments.

The main difference is that investment trusts are themselves companies in which you buy shares. So you are really investing directly in the shares of the Investment Trust company, rather than indirectly through an open-ended Fund such as a Unit Trust (which buys more direct investments as more people step in to pool their money).

Because these share prices are affected in part by supply and demand, their value can fluctuate more often than units in unit trusts. As you'd expect, Investment Trusts offer different levels of risk, depending on the investments they choose. Some focus on capital growth with very little income from dividends; others invest for a steady income from dividends with some chance of capital growth.

An Investment Trust can sometimes be an attractive option if the Investment Manager's strategy is innovative or unusual. But please remember that Investment Trusts involve a bit more risk than the Funds you buy via a Unit Trust.

HOW CAN A CHILD HOLD AN INVESTMENT TRUST

Child Trust Fund aside, children are too young to hold the investments described here in their own names. For this reason we invest in them using what is known as a Bare Trust.

This is a legal trust, under which you (as the trustee) owns the investment, but it is accepted that the investment is for the benefit of your child. When the investment is sold, the child pays tax on any gains has made.

The investment legally transfers to the child on reaching 18 – by which time *The Pocket Money Plan* should have helped create enough wisdom to know what to do with the money.

NATIONAL SAVINGS

National Savings and Investments (NS&I) are extremely safe because they are issued by the government and backed by HM Treasury. In effect, you are lending your money to the Government, so National Savings are similar to Gilts.

Though NS&I offer a range of different investments, the two most applicable to saving for children are Premium Bonds and Children's Bonds.

1. PREMIUM BONDS

When you invest in Premium Bonds you are allocated a series of numbers, one for each £1 invested. Instead of receiving interest payments, you have the chance to win tax-free prizes.

WHO IS ELIGIBLE TO INVEST IN THE BOX?

Anyone over 16. For those under 16, they can be bought on behalf of the child by parents, guardians, grandparents or great grandparents.

WHAT KINDS OF INVESTMENT CAN YOU PUT INSIDE THE BOX?

Premium Bonds are slightly peculiar in that they don't use one of the five main direct investments detailed in Chapter five. They are more similar to Gilts because you are lending your money to the government – but they operate entirely differently.

IS THERE A MINIMUM OR MAXIMUM AMOUNT THAT YOU CAN INVEST?

The minimum is £100, or £50 by monthly standing order, which provides 100 Bond numbers and, therefore, 100 chances of winning a prize. You can hold up to £30,000 of bonds.

HOW CAN YOU ACCESS YOUR MONEY?

Whenever you like, by contacting NS&I. You will always get back what you invested.

WHEN WILL INCOME BE PAID?

Only if you win! As well as the two £1 million jackpots you can win anything from £50 to £100,000 for each Bond number you hold. Each month's prize Fund is equal to a month's interest on the total value of all eligible bonds. You can see this rate at Post Offices or by looking at www.nsandi.com. The odds of winning (as at July 08) were 24,000 to 1. It would be nice to think that with average luck you could get something close to the return you'd get in the building society, but this is speculation. You could win a million or you could get nothing.

HOW WILL PROFITS BE TAXED?

Returns from Premium Bonds are tax-free.

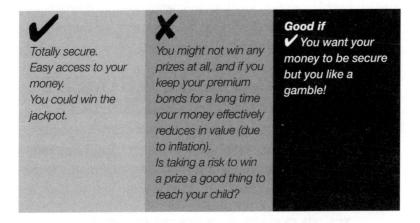

✔	✖	**Good if**
Totally secure. Easy access to your money. You could win the jackpot.	You might not win any prizes at all, and if you keep your premium bonds for a long time your money effectively reduces in value (due to inflation). Is taking a risk to win a prize a good thing to teach your child?	✔ You want your money to be secure but you like a gamble!

CHILDREN'S BONUS BONDS

Children's Bonus Bonds are a lump sum investment available from National Savings & Investments. They were introduced in 1991, initially with an investment limit of £1,000. Backed by the Treasury, they offer guaranteed interest rates when held for five years.

WHO IS ELIGIBLE TO INVEST IN THE BOX?

Anyone aged 16 or over can make an investment for the benefit of someone under 16. The child is the legal owner of the money, but control of the investment is given to the adult.

WHAT KINDS OF INVESTMENT CAN BE PUT INSIDE THE BOX?

Like Premium Bonds, Children's Bonus Bonds are slightly peculiar in that they don't involve one of the five main direct investments. They are more similar to Gilts because you are lending your money to the government – but they operate entirely differently.

IS THERE A MINIMUM OR MAXIMUM AMOUNT YOU CAN INVEST?

The bonds are available in issues and each has its own rate of return. You can invest in as many issues as you like, up to £3,000 per issue for each child. The minimum investment is £25. There are, on average, four issues per year.

HOW CAN YOU ACCESS YOUR MONEY?

You can cash in your investment at any time but, to qualify for

bonuses, the Bonds have to be held for five years or until the child is 21. No interest is earned if a Bond is cashed in within a year of purchase.

WHEN WILL INCOME BE PAID?

At the end of the five-year period – but it is added to your investments as it goes along. Each Bond earns a fixed rate of interest for five years and, on the fifth anniversary, a bonus is added. The bonus is fixed when you apply for the Bond, so you know exactly what the investment will be worth at the end of the term.

Here's an example.
Mum invests £3,000 in Children's Bonus Bond Issue 20 for her daughter. The sum earns compound interest of 2.95 per cent per year for the first five years (£468.91). On the fifth anniversary the investment earns a 5.16 per cent bonus of the original investment value (£154.80). So after five years, the initial £3,000 investment would be worth £3,623.71. Source: NS&I, August 2007

HOW WILL PROFITS BE TAXED?

They are tax-free, even if the child becomes a taxpayer. There is no tax for parents to pay either, and the £100 rule doesn't apply to Children's Bonus Bonds.

Children's Bonus Bonds

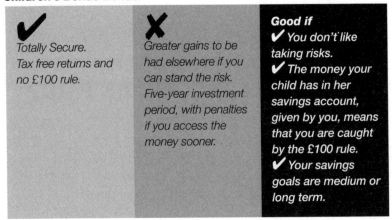

✔
Totally Secure.
Tax free returns and
no £100 rule.

✗
Greater gains to be
had elsewhere if you
can stand the risk.
Five-year investment
period, with penalties
if you access the
money sooner.

Good if
✔ You don't like
taking risks.
✔ The money your
child has in her
savings account,
given by you, means
that you are caught
by the £100 rule.
✔ Your savings
goals are medium or
long term.

FRIENDLY SOCIETY INVESTMENTS

Friendly Societies are basically Life Assurance companies with
some special tax privileges. This allows them to offer some unique
investment products, that come with tax breaks.

However, Friendly Societies have more than this one string to
their bow. Many now offer unit trusts, OEICS, investment trusts,
and life assurance. Most have Child Trust Fund products as the
mainstay of their business. All of these are covered elsewhere, so
we will just look at the Friendly Society investment product not
available elsewhere. It goes under many guises. Some call it a 'Baby

Bond', but the technical term is a Friendly Society Savings Plan.

This is a regular savings plan, set up for a minimum of ten years, and funded by regular payments (or occasionally a lump sum). The aim is to provide a tax-free lump sum at some point in the future.

WHO IS ELIGIBLE TO BUY OR INVEST IN THE BOX?

Parents can invest on behalf of children under 18. The maximum age for taking out a friendly society policy is 70.

WHAT KIND OF INVESTMENTS CAN BE PUT INSIDE THE BOX?

There are three kinds: 'With Profits' Funds, Equity-Based Funds, and Deposit Funds.

1. 'WITH PROFITS'

As with other Funds, you buy some units from the Investment Manager's big Box that then go into your smaller Box. But instead of getting all of the growth added to the value of your 'unit', the Fund Manager declares an Annual Bonus.

Once this bonus has been added to the value of your units it can't be taken away. By giving you a bonus rather than the actual growth, the Fund Manager can decide to hold back some of the profits so that, when times get tough, some of the 'saved' money is left over to provide a welcome boost. In this way your returns are smoothed.

'With Profits' Funds are the basis of most friendly society savings plans.

2. EQUITY-BASED FUNDS

Here, the Fund strategy is to produce returns similar to those of a particular Index of the Stock Market.

3. DEPOSIT FUNDS

Quite simply, the Friendly Society invests your money in a deposit account with a leading bank or building society.

IS THERE A MINIMUM OR MAXIMUM AMOUNT THAT YOU CAN INVEST?

You are limited to £270 a year per person (£25 a month) for all friendly society policies combined. Some friendly societies will allow you to pay this as a lump sum, adding together the value of all premiums due over the term of the policy (normally 10 years). Parents can invest £270 a year for each child under 18, as well as for themselves.

HOW DO YOU ACCESS YOUR MONEY?

Policies are usually set up for ten years, with penalties if you want your money back sooner. Doing this can also mean that you pay tax on any gain at your normal rate of income tax.

WHEN WILL INCOME BE PAID?

Any income stays inside the Fund.

HOW WILL PROFITS BE TAXED?

The Fund Manger pays tax on the dividends gained, but this is dealt with inside the Fund. If you keep your investment for ten years, the lump sum returned to you is tax-free.

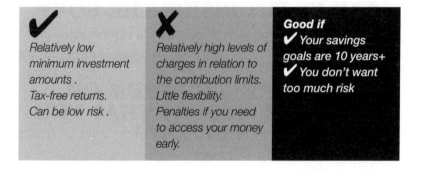

✔
Relatively low
minimum investment
amounts .
Tax-free returns.
Can be low risk .

✗
Relatively high levels of
charges in relation to
the contribution limits.
Little flexibility.
Penalties if you need
to access your money
early.

Good if
✔ Your savings
goals are 10 years+
✔ You don't want
too much risk

STAKEHOLDER PENSIONS

No, I haven't gone mad. Yes, your child can have a pension.

WHO IS ELIGIBLE TO BUY OR INVEST IN THE BOX?

Anyone, including any child. They can start their investment from birth.

A parent, guardian or grandparent can set up a stakeholder pension and pay the contributions for any number of children under 18. After that the child can start making his own contributions. If you happen to be buying a stakeholder for someone else's child, you must tell the child's parents to ensure that he or she contributes to only one stakeholder pension in any tax year.

WHAT KIND OF INVESTMENTS CAN BE PUT INSIDE THE BOX?

As with Unit Trusts there is a wide range of Investment and Fund Managers offering Funds to suit all kinds of attitude to risk.

IS THERE A MINIMUM OR MAXIMUM AMOUNT THAT YOU CAN INVEST?

A child can contribute up to £2,808 a year. He or she can get tax relief on this (at the basic rate of tax), so when this is added £3,600 is actually invested. You can pay this amount on an annual basis or the equivalent every month. Or you can pay as little as £20 per month.

You can increase, decrease, stop and start payments at any time. You can also transfer to another company without any penalty.

HOW CAN YOU ACCESS YOUR MONEY?

You can't – not until you retire, at any rate. For all children this is eons away!

WHEN WILL INCOME BE PAID?

Nothing doing until your child retires. The investment is locked away until then.

HOW WILL PROFITS BE TAXED?

The tax advantages of pension funds are complex, but it's fair to say that any gains you make in interest or investment growth will be treated more favourably by the tax man than they would be if you were invested in another investment product – for example a unit trust.

There's a second benefit: when you contribute to a pension plan, the tax man rewards you for investing in pensions by immediately adding money to the amount you've paid. For example, if you pay basic rate tax he'll add 24 per cent to anything you've contributed, and the insurance company will automatically add this to your fund. If you're a higher rate tax payer you get 40 per cent added. This time the insurance company deals with the 'basic' bit, while you can get the 'higher' bit when you do your tax return.

Of course tax laws change, and no one knows what they'll be in 50 years' time!

WHY A PENSION FOR A CHILD CAN MAKE SENSE

Setting up a pension scheme for a child isn't as crazy as you might think. The miracle of compound interest means that small investments made now could grow into very significant amounts after 50 or more years. But only consider it if you are lucky enough to have all the normal stuff covered: college or university, a car, a gap year, and so on.

The fact that the pension Fund is 'locked up' throughout your child's working life isn't a bad thing. It will still be an asset, enabling him or her to use their resources in other areas.

Money at retirement might not be totally sorted, but at least it will be further along the line than otherwise. And if you really can start at birth the value of the Fund at retirement could be colossal! Here's an example of how it could turn out.

WHAT YOUR CHILD'S PENSION FUND MIGHT BE WORTH AT AGE 65

	Age contributions start			
	Birth	**Age 10**	**Age18**	**Age 65**
Monthly net	£23.33	£42.50	£69.00	**£250,000**
contributions				
and projected	£46.66	£84.50	£137.50	**£500,000**
Fund values	£93.50	£170.00	£275.50	**£1m**
	£140.00	£253.50	£412.66	**£1.5m**
	£186	£338	£550	**£2m**
	£233	£422	£689	**£2.5m**

Of course these figures are only illustrative. The returns here are based on an investment return of seven per cent a year, and an annual managements charge of one per cent of the Fund. It also assumes that all payments due until retirement are made, and that tax rules don't change.

Source: Scottish Widows.

HOW TO CHOOSE WHAT'S BEST FOR YOU

So far you have a good overview of the different investment options (direct and indirect) open to you, and how they work. You can compare this to your own savings objectives, and your attitude to risk.

But once you decide that a CTF, say, or a Unit Trust sounds like your best bet, this is only half the battle. Now you need to find the one most likely to help YOU (and perhaps your child) amass that Money Mountain. To do this, you need to ask four questions.

TAX TIP

For many grandparents, inheritance tax (IHT) is a worry. But investment products that allow regular payments (from earned income) are a great way to avoid paying this tax while helping grandchildren. This is because they are not treated as 'gifts' which can carry tax liabilities. Because IHT is a complicated area it is always best to seek out professional legal and financial advice.

1. WHAT ARE THE CHARGES?

It doesn't take a rocket scientist to work out that if you get a five per cent return, but the investment product costs you five per cent, you've made zilch.

Promise yourself you will shop around with a minimum of three different providers for any investment product that you are thinking of choosing. Make sure you know, up front, all of the charges involved with each investment. These should be clearly outlined in the 'key facts' or 'key features' documents you will receive. They should tell you all the nitty gritty, in plain English, and should be available to you before you make your investment. In each case, it's a wad of paper you can't afford to ignore.

You should also receive projections of the amount you might expect to get back from the money you invest. Part of this includes a 'reduction in yield' figure – the amount by which your possible profit will be affected by the charges involved.

As with everything in life, the cheapest is not always be the best, but knowing the costs is the right starting point.

2. WHAT IS THE COMPANY'S TRACK RECORD?

There are actually two track records you're interested in. One is the reputation of the company providing the Box (Investment Product, if you prefer); the other is the reputation of the Fund Manager who makes the investments that might go inside your Box.

THE COMPANY'S REPUTATION

First off, in most cases, you want a household name. If you invest money with someone you've never heard of, or who doesn't have a significant presence online or in the financial press, you are already further up the Risk Slope then you might want to be.

There are plenty of industry awards. Have a look at the company's website and see if they've won any. Most will proudly display their achievements somewhere.

An award from Independent Financial Advisers (IFAs) is a good sign. These guys deal with investment and life assurance companies day in, day out and very quickly get to know which are good and which are not.

Any recognition for providing good service is a big plus point. Most of these companies are huge and difficult to deal with (trust me, I have a lot of experience with this). A recent award for customer service is some indication that, for time being at least, you won't face a thousand different telephone options every time you call them, before eventually getting through to someone in Outer Mongolia.

THE FUND MANAGER'S REPUTATION

'Past performance is not necessarily a guide to the future', goes the old saying, and rightly so. Investment or Fund Managers are only as good as their last gain, and this could change at any moment.

What past performance does do is give you some idea of the pedigree of people involved in running the Fund you are considering (though of course there are no guarantees that this will continue). So use the internet to the full. www.morningstar. co.uk and www.trustnet.com are just two among many who review the relative performance of different Funds. They also rate individual Funds, mostly on a 1-5 star basis.

Make sure that you look at the Fund Fact Sheet for any Fund that you are considering, available online from the company whose Fund you are trying to assess. It will show exactly where the Fund Manager is currently investing, and tell you in detail what the strategy is. Most importantly, it will show you recent performance.

Funds tend to be grouped in segments called quartiles, which might as well be called quarters. If your Fund is in the top quartile, that means it has performed in the top 25 per cent of Funds with similar strategies. If it's fourth quartile then at least 75 per cent of similar Funds have given better performance. Look at the quartile performance not just over the last year but further back too (the usual time periods are three, five and ten years). You are looking for consistency over a long period. 'Flash in the Pan' performance is the least likely to be repeated.

Dectiles (divisions of a tenth) take this analysis even further. A Fund in the top dectile is in the top 10 per cent of performers. Saddle yourself with one in the bottom dectile and you'll have found yourself a duffer.

3. HOW APPROACHABLE IS THE COMPANY?

You're highly unlikely to find an investment provider that your child can visit, but you might hope to get regular correspondence. It's crucial in generating discussion with your child.

Sadly, few investment companies are geared up to write to your child in an appropriate way. Letters are likely to be the same for all their investors, young and old. So try to decipher them for your kids to involve them in the (hopefully) positive effects of investing.

Look at the company's online capabilities too. It's going to be important to your child to 'see' your money as it grows. You should be able to sign on securely to track progress.

Some financial experts will tell you that approachability is not a worthy consideration, and that the return on your money is the 'be all and end all'. I disagree. Yes, growing money is your main objective, but the powerful secondary one is teaching your child as you go. My advice is to find an investment company which can help you do this.

4. ARE THERE ANY EXTRAS?

Free gifts are not that widespread when it comes to investment products. The most you're likely to see is a product branded with a cartoon or storybook character. Be very careful. Whilst this branding may create some initial interest for your child, he or she will soon grow out of it within the minimum likely term of five

years. Pay attention to the charges and past performance instead.

Be equally cautious about extra 'bells and whistles' added to the Investment Product – for example, introductory rates that drop like a stone the minute your back is turned, or the promise to keep you updated on the progress of your investment for free (it already is free – you only have to ask). These will carry a price tag and, unless they offer something you definitely need, you are best to go without.

THE MOMENT OF RECKONING

If these four questions give you the confidence to make a final choice, then good for you. Go for it!

If you have any reservations whatsoever, it's best to ask for help. Your money was hard-earned, after all.

FINDING A FINANCIAL ADVISER

It's fine to say that investing gives you a worldwide staff of thousands. But that's a lot of people. Sometimes it's best to get yourself a recruitment consultant to help you decide which of these workers is worth their wages. More often than not the best person to help you will be a Financial Adviser.

There are several different kinds and you need to know about this before you go looking. Some advisers charge a fee for their services – normally an hourly rate, but sometimes in relation to the amount of money they have advised you about. Others don't charge you directly, but are paid a sum (called as 'commission') by the company they have helped you become a customer of.

Your first question should always be: 'What type of adviser are you?'

Now let's look at what the answers actually mean.

'I AM INDEPENDENT.'

These guys offer savings and investment products from the whole of the marketplace. There are regulations to ensure they consider your needs and objectives, so that they can match you with the most suitable product – should you require one at all. They will give you options about how you can pay them for their expertise, but this will always include payment by fee, rather than commission, if that is what you would prefer.

'I AM A WHOLE OF MARKET ADVISER.'

Essentially the same as independents except that they work on a commission-only basis. You can't pay them a fee for their advice, even if you would like to.

'I AM MULTI-TIED.'

Unable to survey the whole market; instead, they offer products from a particular range of firms.

'I AM SINGLE-TIED.'

Like the multi guys, they can't survey the whole market to find the product that is best for you. They only advise on products from one provider.

If all of that's not confusing enough, there are also financial advisory firms operating a combination of different types of adviser. The message is clear: make sure you know who you are dealing with. The adviser should always give you some documents about this up front. As a minimum you should also get:

A business card

A document called 'Key Facts About Our Services'

A document entitled 'Terms of Business' (or sometimes 'Client Agreement')

If these documents aren't offered to you then the adviser is not complying with very strict rules, set by the Financial Services Authority (FSA), under which he or she is regulated.

SO WHICH ONE IS THE BEST?

It largely depends on what is on offer in your local community, but I would suggest that an Independent Adviser or, failing that, a Whole of Market Adviser is your best bet. Their need to survey every company and product to best meet your needs means that they work in your best interests and can have no bias in their selection. With the other advisers you can't be so sure.

Of course, choosing which type of Adviser you would like is only half the battle. You've then got to find a good one.

In my experience a personal recommendation is always worth listening to. Friends and family may have experiences of local advisers, good and bad, so do a quick survey. If you have a solicitor or accountant, ask them to recommend someone. Remember, their reputation is on the line if they recommend you to a duffer. So if they are happy to suggest someone, pay heed.

Failing all that, there is a lot of help online if you do a bit of digging. Here are a few helpful sites:

Find a local Adviser, plus lots of investment advice:
www.investmentuk.org

Industry body set up to promote the benefits of independent
financial advice in the UK, including finding a local Adviser:
www.unbiased.co.uk

Find a maximum of seven IFAs in a postcode area (so not always
as comprehensive as it might be):
www.searchifa.co.uk

TIME TO MOVE ON!

And that, is the wonderful world of savings and investments. I told you, didn't I? It's not nearly as complicated as you might have imagined. Yes, the possibilities are numerous but if you are clear on your objectives, your attitude to risk and your timescales you CAN choose which investments are likely to be best for you and for your children.

Making the decision to start *The Pocket Money Plan* could make an extraordinary difference to your child's life. And without a doubt, bringing your child up with a knowledge of saving and investments is a huge advantage that one day maybe used to give a great deal of financial security.

There is just one more battle to face, but it might be your toughest yet! You've tackled Giving and Saving. Now it's time to face the big boys – it's time to talk about Spending.

Every product is a
bait by means of which
the individual tries
to entice the essence
of the other person,
his money

KARL MARX

"I was going to buy him a Bob the Builder
DVD but these Polish chaps are so much
cheaper."

CHAPTER SEVEN

SPENDING

T his chapter offers a practical system to help you bring up your child to spend wisely. It is not a skill children are born with, and it's a sad fact that the modern world makes it harder than it was for any previous generation to develop that skill. But develop it children must, and I will show you that by 'Banishing the Brands' and 'Monitoring' your child can become a Successful Shopper.

THE MESS WE'RE IN

If spending were an Olympic sport, most children could realistically vie for a place on the national team. Their talent, it would seem, knows no bounds.

This isn't altogether their fault. Targeted by literally millions of marketing messages on TV, in magazines, online and even via mobile phones, and surrounded by images promoting the 'Want it, gotta have it' way of life, many of them know little else.

But the results of being a slave to the marketers are that we get into a quite astonishing amount of debt.

TOTAL UK DEBT

£1.44bn	total UK personal debt by the end of May 2008
8%	growth in personal debt since May 2007 – a £107billion increase
£233bn	total consumer credit lending to individuals, May 2008
7%	increase in consumer credit since May 2007
£57,941	average household debt in the UK (including mortgages)
£30,394	average owed by every UK adult (including mortgages)
£4,900	average consumer borrowing via credit cards, motor and retail finance deals, overdrafts and unsecured personal loans, May 2008

Source: Credit Action, July 2008

TODAY IN THE UK

Consumers will borrow an additional **£293m**

Consumers will pay **£258m** in interest

The average household debt will increase by over **£11.75**

424 mortgage possession claims will be issued

408 landlord possession claims will be issued

282 people today will be declared insolvent or bankrupt*

74 properties will be repossessed**

The Citizen's Advice Bureau will deal with **6,600** debt problems

A third of all groceries will end up in the dustbin

Source: Credit Action, July 2008

The Pocket Money Plan

*KPMG estimate this will increase to 356 people a day by the end of 2008. That's one person declared insolvent or bankrupt every four minutes. **The Council of Mortgage lenders estimates this will increase to 123 a day before the end of 2008.*

I don't know about you, but I find these figures pretty terrifying. There is not a shred of doubt that spending habits in the UK need to change. We cannot leave to chance the possibility that our children will grow up to be as reckless as the adults responsible for these shocking figures.

Maybe we shouldn't be over critical. Today's adults, who are responsible for almost all of the UK's debt, are the first generation in history to encounter a consumer society on a grand scale. Just 60 years ago our parents and grandparents were dealing with the deprivations of war, rationing, the austerity of the Fifties, and the fact that there was no widespread access to credit. The shops were shut on Sundays and Wednesday afternoons, Tesco was years in the future, and the mail order market consisted of three or four catalogue brands. On top of all that, most of the stuff on the shelves of our shops today hadn't even been invented.

Compare this with the speed, choice and temptation of today's instant gratification culture. Everything happens at 90mph; our children don't know what a world without fast food tastes like, or how it feels to have to rely on 'snail mail' for the answer to a question that can a search engine can deliver in 0.6 seconds. No

wonder that, when they want something, they want it NOW. And although we parents feel we are doing our children no favours by funding their over-reliance on 'stuff', we seem almost frightened to stand up and say, 'No!' The consumer paradise is controlling us, rather than the other way round.

Few of us, it seems, can cope. Unable to decide what to buy and what to leave alone, we go, quite literally, wild in the aisles. How else can we explain the fact that a third of supermarket food gets chucked straight in the bin?*

And if it's been hard for many adults to keep their heads, what is in store for the next generation? Because today's children face an even more intense world than the one their parents grew up in. And whilst history may have dealt our children a difficult hand in this respect, there is time to make sure they develop more easily the skills that we ourselves had to learn the hard way.

Source: Credit Action

THE MARSHMALLOW EXPERIMENT

Back in the Sixties a researcher sat a group of four year-olds in a room and offered them each a marshmallow. The deal was that they could it eat

The Pocket Money Plan

straight away. However, he explained that he was about to leave the room and if they were willing to wait until he got back he would give them an extra marshmallow.

Some of the children scoffed their treat immediately. Others went to great lengths to control themselves (covering their eyes, singing to themselves, going to sleep) and were able to resist the temptation.

So what? Well, the data gathered years later about these same children showed a miraculous difference between those who were willing to delay gratification, and those who weren't. Now teenagers, not only were they, in general, 'more popular, adventurous, confident and dependable,' – they got better grades in school*

It seems that the ability to wait for want we want is a good skill to develop, and one which says much more about how we'll turn out later in life than we might have expected.

The same psychologists have also found that children who get too many material things have low esteem and self-worth.

It seems that they begin to define themselves in terms of what they have, rather than who they are. On the basis that someone will always have more, this is dangerous territory.

Source: Emotional Intelligence, Daniel Goleman

AFFLUENZA

affluenza, n. a painful, contagious, socially transmitted condition of overload, debt, anxiety and waste resulting from the dogged pursuit of more

Research by some psychologists of note has identified a modern psychological phenomenon known as 'affluenza'*
Perhaps the most worrying of its effects is the development of a false sense of entitlement and the loss of future motivation.
If children grow up getting, they become used to getting. If they grow up getting for free, then by adulthood they have developed a psyche that tells them: 'I am entitled to stuff. There is no downside for me in getting everything I want. Because I am entitled I shouldn't have to work for it.'
The evidence for this mindset is everywhere. And it doesn't take a psychologist to point out that if we feel entitled to something, our power to appreciate it is reduced. That sense of entitlement affects our ability to enjoy what we have now, and to be hopeful and excited by what we might be able to afford in the future.
Do we really want to raise children who value nothing? Let's make sure our children grow up different.

Source: Affluenza, 2002, by John de Graaf, David Wann and Thomas H Naylor

HOW TO MAKE YOUR CHILD A SUCCESSFUL SHOPPER

If you've followed *The Pocket Money Plan* so far, you are already half way there. By insisting on Giving and Saving first, you have shifted the balance away from 'me'. The fact that the money is earned means there can be no false sense of entitlement. All that remains is to help your child spend the contents of the Spend pot.

Let's imagine that, instead of being some boring financial/money type person, I am a celebrity chef. Let me tell you about my latest mouth-watering recipe.

SUCCESSFUL SHOPPERS

INGREDIENTS

1 willing or unwilling child (willing is better)

1 set of Money Pots and a *The Pocket Money Plan*

An adult role model

The courage to show them your own shopping habits

Every ounce of patience you can muster

METHOD

● Place your child in a cold place (known as 'the real world') and impose a Spending Embargo until further notice.

● When he or she has cooled, tell them this is because you will be no longer giving him stuff for free. Outline clearly the Principles of

the Pocket Money Plan. This may initially taste quite bitter, but do not use sugar to sweeten your message.

● Place spend fund in Money Pot. Freeze access, until further notice. Consider lock and key if needed.

● Spend time letting child cook in its own juices. Cooking time will differ by age, experience and the amount by which he/she kicks up a stink. For younger children, one week without spending may be enough. For older children, a month may be required. Or it may take longer still. Don't be tempted to rub salt in by entering into constant discussions. The end result is best if allowed to stew gently.

● Take courage (that's yours) and allow your child to Survey your Shopping.

● Show how you 'Banish the Brands' and 'Monitor the Market'.

● Once your child has mastered the basics, take Spend Pot from freezer and let him or her taste some financial freedom.

● Enjoy!

SO, WHAT'S GOING ON IN THIS STRANGE RECIPE, AND WHY WILL IT WORK?

IMPOSE A SPENDING EMBARGO

This is a break between the old way and the new. Your child needs this time to begin to grasp a new concept: the difference between

'What I need' and 'What I want'. Because he or she is only young, and hasn't had to think about such things before, this will take a while. He or she may well have been so used to saying, 'I want it' (because it was free anyway), that he/she isn't sure what he/she really wants. Allow the brain the time to process the change.

Please resist the temptation to step in at the first whiff of the need to go without. The embargo will do no harm whatsoever. Sorry, but you have to be cruel to be kind.

Let the child know that, after the embargo has passed, when things are needed, you'll help work out how he or she (not you) is going to pay for them. And I tell you; a miraculous thing will happen. While you go shopping during the embargo, your child may try to convince you he or she can't live without the 'stuff' he or she sees. But when, later, he or she is spending their own hard-earned cash, he or she will be a lot more discerning.

NO MORE STUFF FOR FREE

Giving your child stuff for free is psychologically proven to reduce his or her ability to appreciate it. It may even make them ill (see Affluenza, p181). What's certain is that, it limits the ability to assess the value of money and the good feelings that can come from earning.

It's the same with grown-ups. If there's a free bar at a party, and you're not driving, it's human nature to drink more. For your child, substitute 'drink' for 'stuff'. If he or she is to develop the skill to become a Successful Shopper, and to savour the metaphorical glass

of champers rather than knock it back, the free bar has to close.

FREEZE SPEND POT ACCESS

The key problem in today's consumer culture is the overwhelming power of choice. Bombarded with marketing messages and endless possibilities, we don't know if we are coming or going half the time. Distinguishing between our needs and our wants is the way out of this maze – and being good at it is crucial. It gives us a basis on which to make choices in what would otherwise be an endless opportunity to consume.

All of which sounds fine. But it won't stop your child nearly driving you insane because you are not allowing him to buy anything. That's why you need patience.

ALLOW HIM TO SURVEY YOUR SHOPPING

You are your child's first and best role model. Which is why you must now summon every ounce of courage and start to talk to him about your own spending habits.

In fact, this chatter needs to become a habit. You have between now and until your child leaves home to teach him or her to be a successful shopper, and every chance you get needs to be grabbed with both hands. You'll get used to it eventually.

Explain to your child how you spend money. Everyone will have a different view on how far to take this, but the important point is to show how you deal with the real world, and make decisions accordingly. If you haven't bought something because you can't afford it, tell them this too – there's no shame in it. Back up your discussions with practical exercises – for example, getting them to help stick to a budget during the weekly scrum-down at the supermarket.

You have three main behaviours to demonstrate. The first is to separate everything you buy into 'needs' and 'wants', and discuss your reasoning with your child. This helps him or her develop arguments in his own head which he can use when it's his turn to do the buying. The second is to help your child see through marketing hype. And the third is to seek out the best value.

BANISH THE BRANDS

It is shopping suicide to assume that the biggest brand (with the biggest price tag) is always going to offer the biggest benefit. Sometimes the only difference between one widget and another is the strength of its marketing campaign.

To become Successful Shoppers you and your child need to Banish the Brands from your shopping baskets unless you have assessed them in relation to their cheaper cousins and found them to be, hand on heart, worth the extra.

A good rule of thumb for that assessment is durability. The longer an item is likely to last, the more likely it is that you should pay more for a well known brand. If an item is likely to last no time

at all, try the cheaper alternatives first. Of course there are times – generally when you're considering expensive, long-lasting items – when you should opt for the best you can afford. But it is not always so and therefore you need to do your research.

Take the humble baked bean. If you buy the cheapest you can find and they taste awful, you can always try the next best next week, and so on, until you find the quality you are happy with. You may well end up with the most expensive brand but at least now your spending is informed. You've not become a slave to the adverts.

Don't under-estimate the money to be saved in this way. *The Mail on Sunday* recently reported that a student could save £400 a year by banishing brands from the weekly food shop – a handy sum to reduce an overdraft or fund a few nights down the Student Union bar. And that's just one person.

MONITOR THE MARKET

You can approach small items using experience or, as with our baked beans example, trial and error. But for bigger items (I'll leave you to decide what this amount might be), you need to ask some pre-purchase questions.

Just like choosing an investment, a major purchase of any kind should only be made after you've studied at least three different possibilities. Your short list should consist of one of the cheapest versions of the item on the market, one mid price, and one top-of-the-range version. Suddenly, as with the beans, you can compare.

The trick is to stand back and ask yourself: what are the features and benefits that this item offers me, and how do they compare to the price being charged? Do you really need these features? If the answer is no, then you are wasting your money.

It almost certainly wasn't easy but, by now, your child should know something about 'needs' and 'wants', value for money, and shopping around. And he or she will be champing at the bit to deal some dosh.

The final step will help put your child's newfound wisdom into practice.

HOW TO BUILD A BUDGET

Remember bottom-up financial planning?

Our 'needs' are the everyday expenses of living. Our 'wants' are the cream at the top. The first job is to make sure we have enough money to fund the needs. Only then can we enjoy the bit that's left over.

This is the essence of budgeting – and it's a skill your child will benefit from for the rest of his life.

Even the youngest children can have a budget of sorts. By the time your child is a teenager (when the Spend fund must cover a lot more than 'treats'), he or she needs to be building a budget on the same day and hour that you hand over the cash.

It's not difficult and it needn't take long.

continued page 194

USE THE WEB TO SAVE MONEY

SHOPBOTS

This is short for shopping robot – a website that uses a search engine to work out which retailer is likely to give you the best price on an item such as a book, DVD, major electrical item or car. There are many, many shopbots, some generalist such as www.kelkoo.co.uk or www.shopping.com, and some which specialise, such as www.media-pricer.co.uk for DVDs and CDs, or www.mysupermarket.co.uk for groceries.

CASHBACK SITES

Another option (or use both and compare results) is a cashback site. These are set up to make their money from advertising. They list different retailers, and then get paid by the retailer if you click through to their website. The cashback site then shares this payment with you. Good examples include www.rpoints.co.uk and www.topcashback.co.uk. There are definite savings to be made!

CONSUMER ADVICE

If you're really keen, www.moneysavingexpert.com and www.fool.com are stuffed with ideas and reports to help improve your buying power.

FIVE STEPS TO BUILDING A BUDGET WITH YOUR CHILD

1. ITEMS TO BUY

Get your child to write down all of the items that might be bought (with prices) before next Pocket Money payday.

2. SOCIAL EVENTS

List any social events coming up which might involve spending money. Guesstimate the cost.

3. NEED OR WANT?

Split the above lists into needs and wants.

4. CAN HE/SHE AFFORD IT?

Tally the cost of the 'need' items. If there's any money left over, compare the costs of the 'want' items to the amount of remaining cash

5. FIND THE BEST VALUE

See if it's possible to Banish the Brands and Monitor the Market to find the best deal.

The idea is to get your child into the habit of writing down the

continued page 196

TEACH YOUR CHILD TO SEE THROUGH THE HYPE

Here's an extravagant but hard-hitting method to teach your child about value for money.

Suppose you are at the cinema. Before you go in your child asks for a bag of Maltesers and a Coke, upon which a teenage assistant asks you for a sum that genuinely drops your jaw.

You mention that £5.50 is an awful lot for a few choccies and a fizzy drink, but your child is under ten, and can't grasp the concept too well: 'Yeah, so what?' Clearly, a lecture isn't going to work.

So on the way home you go to the supermarket and invite your child to spend £5.50 on sweets and drinks. It takes a while. He/she looks at specific branded sweets, and compares the prices with own brand ones. He/she discovers the difference between buying a bottle and a can. He/she notices a 'buy two, get one free' deal. And when finally finished, he/she can't believe how much more has been bought. OK, it cost you. But your child is beginning to understand.

Try it, you'll be amazed!

rough cost of everything he or she might want to buy (or, if older, to use a spreadsheet). Later on you can both keep track of what things actually cost.

The budgeting process gives clear guidelines of what can and cannot be bought, based on his or her own assessment of 'needs' and 'wants'. The child can then make the best of the resources by looking for good value. Remember, the shorter the time an item is likely to last, the more important it is to start cheap!

If your son or daughter finds an item is cheaper than expected, happy days! Maybe he or she can afford something else besides – or, better still, keep it in the Spend Pot for a while!

There are plenty of budgeting suggestions and downloads on www.pocketmoneyplan.co.uk.

WHAT ABOUT THE UNEXPECTED?

The best thing about knowing where you are with your cash is the flexibility to take advantage of opportunities that come your way. There will be times when something crops up that your child hadn't envisaged when building the budget. Fear not! Budgets, like bridges, can be rebuilt.

You do it by reviewing and discussing the 'needs' and 'wants' list. If priorities have changed, and the unplanned event or thing is more important than the original plan, then it can be adjusted

accordingly. Or not. Or, if the money's already spent, he or she can learn the value of keeping money back.

The main thing is, your child is learning to choose.

WHAT IF YOUR CHILD DOESN'T SPEND ALL HIS/HER MONEY?

If the Spend pot consistently fails to empty, it could be that you are being too generous – in which case you might reduce the pocket money, or ask your child to buy more essentials. Otherwise, it's OK for a small surplus to build up – it gives the flexibility to deal with unplanned events. Of course, if you are giving money weekly and there is an item that will only be bought monthly, then you need to take this into account.

WHAT IF YOUR CHILD WOULD PREFER TO SAVE?

If your child makes a good argument for a pressing short-term goal, then fine. But don't allow him or her to do so lightly. *The Pocket Money Plan* is not only about learning to save; it is also about allowing children to enjoy spending, within reason. Encourage your child to reach a balance.

BUDGET EXAMPLES

SIMON, AGE 9

Simon gets £4.50 a week from his parents, in line with the '50p per year' rule of thumb. He hasn't got any agreement to earn extra. He puts 45p in his Give Pot and £1.35 in his Save Pot. That leaves him £2.70 to spend.

His parents pay for most things. He's still little and his only 'extravagance' is at Saturday football, when he likes to buy a drink and sweets. He also likes a footie magazine which comes out every two weeks. Here's his budget:

1. ITEMS TO BUY

Soft drink 60p

Chocolate Bar 50p

Magazine £1.00

2. SOCIAL EVENTS

Parents pay (worth knowing in itself)

3. NEED OR WANT?

Since all are 'wants', all of Simon's money is 'cream at the top'

4. CAN HE AFFORD IT?

Total cost is £2.10 from a Spend Pot of £2.70.

It is fine for him to keep back 60p for another time.

5. FIND THE BEST VALUE

Scope here is limited. He's not yet at the stage where he needs to Banish Brands. He could Monitor the Market by seeing if there is a cheaper magazine that he likes just as much. OK, he could probably find a soft drink and chocolate bar for less, but he is enjoying using his own earned money to treat himself after a game of footie with his mates. That's much more important than saving a few pence. (That's not to say that his Mum shouldn't tell him that he could get them cheaper elsewhere, just so he knows!)

CHRISTINA, AGE 16

Christina's parents give her £32 every four weeks (still 50p a year). She earns an extra £10 a week on average by gardening for neighbours, and £30 more by babysitting two or three times a month. This brings her overall income to around £100 a month.

She puts £10 in her Give Pot and £30 in her Save Pot. She has £60 in her Spending Pot. Her parents pay for a monthly travelcard (which also gets her to school), plus most of her clothes. Christina uses her own money for any additional items of clothing, her toiletries and socialising.

She sits down with her mum to build her budget for the next month.

The Pocket Money Plan

1. ITEMS TO BUY

New mascara £10

Hot drinks at school (20 x 50p) £10

Chocolate! £5

New top £12

Shampoo nearly finished £6

2. SOCIAL EVENTS

Want to see that new film £8

Will probably go to the cinema at least once more £8

Popcorn at the cinema £3

3. NEED OR WANT?

Christina's everyday expenses needs are:

Shampoo £6

Mascara £10

Drinks at school £10

Her 'wants' are:

Chocolate £5

Going to the cinema £16

New Top £12

Popcorn £3

Total potential spend £62

4. CAN SHE AFFORD IT?

Christina is a lucky girl and she has also worked hard, so she can afford her everyday expenses. But she is disappointed to be slightly over budget for her 'Cream at the top'. The new top she has her eye

only just made it into the 'want' rather than 'need' list, and yet it looks like she may have to go without.

But hang on a minute, what about Monitoring the Market and Banishing the Brands?

5. FIND THE BEST VALUE

Christina's mother asks who, in their right mind, would pay ten per cent of their monthly salary on mascara when a quick shufty round Boots reveals at least three different types for £1.99. Christina's £6 one is branded, and on the basis that mascara doesn't last long she needs to start cheap and work her way up. Or at least have a cheap one for everyday use, and the expensive one for special occasions. Same for the £6 shampoo – Banish the Brand and you can get some for £1.49 – a saving of £4.51.

Just by surveying two items in her shopping basket Christina has saved £8.52 – more than enough to justify the top.

It may be that, until now, Christina's mum bought her daughter's shampoo and mascara. She may never have questioned the wisdom of buying what are obviously premium brands. Now that *The Pocket Money Plan* has given her the opportunity to think about it, maybe she'll decide that the six quid shampoo was never that good anyway – it was just what she used to buying. Maybe she didn't even know how much it cost in the first place. She does now.

Christina has two potential cinema trips this month – but it's the school holidays and she will probably want to go more often than this. If she does a little research online she will discover that, for a monthly commitment of £10.99, the cinema will allow her to visit as many times as she likes. This information is not hard to find and the savings are great.

The result? Christina was upset because she wasn't sure she could afford the £12 top – but then she'd already planned to spend £8.52 more than she needed to on shampoo and mascara, and £5.01 more than she needed on the cinema.
Already she is seeing positive benefits of *The Pocket Money Plan*. Encouraged, she is well on her way to becoming a successful shopper!

Debt, n. An ingenious substitute for the chain and whip of the slavedriver.

AMBROSE BIERCE,
THE DEVIL'S DICTIONARY

CHAPTER EIGHT

LEARNING ABOUT LOANS

Children are too young to get credit in the real world – but they still need to learn how debt works. This chapter explains why you might want to lend them money so that they can grasp the basics in a safe environment.

Strange though it may be to read in a book detailing the horrors of personal debt, you should think about lending your child money. Of course it's not ideal. But it's unrealistic to think that children can get to adulthood, and maybe raise a family, without using some form of credit. For example, unless you are extremely well organised and/or extremely rich, a university or college education goes hand in hand with debt. If your child is to become a student then managing credit will be one of the toughest tests to be faced. It's just a fact of life – and one you can prepare his for.

● Cost of student debt				
Cost today	Estimated cost in 5 years	Estimated cost in 12 years	Estimated cost in 15 years	Estimated cost in 18 years
£12,363	£13,900	£16,600	£17,900	£19,200

Source: Childrens Mutual

Cost of student debt: *The 2007 NatWest Student Money Matters survey estimated that the average student leaving a three-year university course in 2007 had a £12,363 debt. This assumes tuition fees of £3,000 a year and living costs for terms lasting eight months. The figures in this chart assume inflation will run at 2.5 per cent a year.*

MANAGING DEBT IS A SKILL

Your child has already learned that saving becomes a habit, and spending wisely is a skill. Debt management is no different. It's a skill that needs to be developed, sooner rather than later. The consequences of failing to repay debt need no elaboration here. So wouldn't you rather be the one to hold his hand should his first steps be a little faltering? That's decided then

.

DID YOU KNOW?

● Over half of England's teenagers are in debt
by the time they are 17

● 90 per cent worry about their money and spending, but tend to think of overdrafts and credit cards as easy ways to spend more than they earn or to buy things they couldn't normally afford

Research: Personal Finance Education Group. Source: Credit Action

DID YOU KNOW?

● There are more credit cards in England than people, according to APACS. At the end of 2006 there were 74.4m credit cards and charge cards compared to 60 million people.

Source: Credit Action

● The biggest cause of stress for most people is money (51 per cent)

Source: Samaritans

HOW TO HANDLE A CHILD ASKING TO BORROW MONEY

You can never lend money without conditions. And the first condition is: is your child a Pocket Money Pro? Can he or she happily split the money three ways, take pride in giving to charity, and never quibble over filling that Save Pot? Most of all, does your child understand the link between earning and work?

If the answer is yes, then he or she is ready for the extra responsibility of borrowing money. But before you hand it over, there are five criteria to consider.

1. WHAT IS THE LOAN FOR?

Since money doesn't grow on trees, it has to be a worthy cause
– which generally means unplanned events.

These are the occasions that present exciting possibilities for your
child, either to have fun or to further his or her education. It could be
a simple day out on the train, or something more significant such as
a school trip, sporting tour or holiday with friends. Events like these
really do appear suddenly sometimes, which makes them hard to
budget or save for. Just try to be sure that you're not funding a last-
minute loan for something which your child could have saved for,
if he or she had bothered. Because if this is the case, then the harsh
lesson of missing out might well be one he or she needs to learn.

Of course it isn't always that simple. Your child may not have
approached you with a request for a loan in the first place. Perhaps
assuming you would pay for the trip, in true pre-Pocket Money
Plan form. Stay strong! You may have been tempted in the past to
splash out for an easy life, but this can't continue.

So this is a time to stop and think. Your only objective is to teach
your child to appreciate the value of money. Should you fund it
all? Should he? Try not to be black and white either way. Even if
he funds as little as ten per cent of a trip himself, the learning
experience could be valuable enough – and it's the experience you
are interested in.

Don't view his need to contribute as harsh; it isn't that at
all. Instead, remember that you are letting your child have the

satisfaction and enjoyment that comes from paying for something. You are teaching your child valuable money behaviour rather than offering a blank cheque, because this is how the real world works.

Oh, and never, ever be talked into lending money to a child who has spent the entire month's pocket money shortly after receiving it. But then, you don't need me to tell you that.

2. OUTLINE YOUR TERMS

You must charge your child interest on the money borrowed. This is how debt really operates, and to encourage your son or daughter to think otherwise it will do him no good at all. Besides, you could be putting the cash in a savings account.

So how much interest? As always with children, it's a balancing act. I'd urge you to be competitive against high street rates. On one hand, you've already taught the need to shop around. On the other hand he or she needs to know that this is a privilege – and that debt isn't cheap. If it becomes a Mickey Mouse exercise, you teach nothing.

3. SET OUT A SMART REPAYMENT SCHEDULE

Use the SMART principle to ensure that a child can pay you back in a Specific, Measurable time (the 'A' for Appropriate you dealt with up front, when deciding whether or not to authorise the loan in the first place).

That repayments are Realistic and Timed is probably most important. Don't set a child up to fail by creating an unrealistically quick timescale. To a certain extent, the longer the pain of repayment can continue (within reason) the more you reinforce the idea that using debt isn't a fun way of managing money.

A really helpful technique is to create a written repayment schedule which shows when he or she has stopped repaying the original loan amount, and when he's started on the interest. It's not about being cruel; you just want him or her to realise that this credit lark isn't easy.

S	**Specific:** *have you set out very clearly how much you will lend and at what interest rate?*
M	**Measurable:** *Are your repayment terms clearly explained and recorded?*
A	**Appropriate:** *Is the purpose of the loan appropriate?*
R	**Realistic:** *Are the terms set out and the repayment schedule realistic, given your child's budget?*
T	**Timed:** *Has a deadline been set for repayment?*

4. DECIDE ON THE EXTRA EARNING

Extra earning will be the foundation of your child's repayment plan because, again, that's how it is in the real world. Decide what jobs are going to be done, and when and how much they are going to be paid, just as you do when your child is earning for his or her Spend or short term Save funds.

It may seem like stating the obvious, but be sure you stick to the repayment schedule. Your heart may warm at the glorious sight of your teenager engaged in worthy employment. Nevertheless – make him or her pay back every last penny. DO NOT let your child off with paying three quarters and then utter that famous parenting cop-out, 'You've done really well, you've learned your lesson'. No he or she hasn't! Does your credit card company ever phone up, congratulate you on paying three quarters of the bill, and promise to cancel the rest? I think not.

In fact, this situation tends to develop in two ways. Either your child will see you as a soft touch or, because he or she knows you won't take the money back, feels unable to ask for your help when it's really needed.

5. NO SECOND CHANCES

For all the right reasons this has to be a one-chance arrangement. If your child borrows from the most competitive bank in his world and doesn't stick to the repayment schedule, do not lend him or her money again for a very, very long time.

MOBILE PHONES

There can be few teenagers who haven't been in debt to their parents over a mobile phone. And that makes them an ideal tool to teach financial responsibility.

Most of us want our older children to have a mobile. But many children burn through their monthly credit within a short time, then carry on regardless. Others, with pay-as-you-go tariffs, never seem to have any credit, which renders the phone almost completely useless.

So why not try your own payment plan, agreeing a monthly sum which you will stump up? At the end of the month you sit down together and work out how many calls have actually been paid for, and how many have busted the price limit – effectively getting your child into debt with the phone company.

Explain that the people at the phone company are much nastier than you. They don't offer credit terms. They simply sue you if you don't pay. Now offer a rescue plan. As with the loan, you must set SMART targets for the interest on the loan, and the repayment terms. Now watch the bill reduce drastically next month.

It's paid off for me once, but it's not a sure fire plan. With kids and mobile phones, nothing can be. But it's more likely to work than an empty promise, which makes it worth a go. It's certainly a more adult response than throwing your child's SIM card away in a fit of fury.

REAL CREDIT

As technology marches on, the world of commerce will come up with more and more ways to persuade your child to spend money. There will soon be cards on the market which mimic credit cards – or which, for those over 16, might even be proper credit cards.

Be wary, but not totally against. Using notes and coins is beneficial, but it's not always practical. Online transactions, for example. And sometimes carrying a lot of cash is not the safest thing.

But plastic needn't mean credit. Many banks and other organisations now offer a pre-payment card, which you load with money and use as a debit card. This is a great idea: no risk of biting off more than you can chew, and it's still safer than carrying cash. But not all these cards are the same. The simpler ones can be used online or in shops, and carry reasonable fees. The more complex ones need monthly memberships, can run out within certain timescales, and charge you for cash machine withdrawals.

So examine any credit or prepayment product with a fine-tooth comb. Think long and hard about the intentions of the company involved. Are they making a fair profit, and treating your child with respect? Or as an unsuspecting consumer they can take for a ride? If you are diligent in these matters, your child will follow your example.

USE DEBT WELL

We all hate debt, with good reason. It costs us money and, for many, it spirals out of control.

Introducing your child to the subject gently may set him or her out on a different path. Dealt with correctly, debt can be an asset, not a liability. It's the inability to control (and repay) debt that causes the trouble – not the debt itself.

Using debt wisely can allow your child to take opportunities in life that might otherwise pass by. Your child can do this if he or she feels confident about how debt works, and understands the steps (and sacrifices) it takes to pay back money that has been borrowed. If he or she can go through life giving debt the respect it deserves, your child can definitely use it to his or her advantage.

"Not the prince meets the princess, prince saves the princess and they live happily ever after. Read me something about investment TOISAs and ISAs."

CHAPTER NINE

JARGON JUGGLER

As I keep saying, saving and investing isn't complicated. It's just that the language is sometimes difficult. This chapter, then, is the naughty corner for definitions. If a word in this book (or elsewhere) has a meaning that isn't immediately clear, you should find it here.

Accumulation units/shares

With some units (in Investment Funds) or shares any income you earn can remain invested, or in other words, it accumulates. The value of the units increases or you are allocated more units or shares.

Annual management charge (AMC)

This is the fee charged by a fund manager once a year. It pays for the cost of managing and administering the investment. The charge can be anything from 0.5%-2% p.a. and the charge is taken from your investments.

Annual report

This lets you know what the fund you are investing in is trying to achieve and shows you how it has performed. The fund manager produces this Report at the end of the financial year.

Assets

This is a way of referring to the direct and/or indirect investments you hold e.g. 'The value of his assets are £x".

Asset allocation

Describes how your money is invested. The idea is to spread your money across a range of different assets and companies in order to diversify. This helps to spread risk.

Authorised investment fund

A unit trust or OEIC that is regulated by the Financial Services Authority (FSA). All unit trusts and OEICs available to investors in the UK are authorised by the FSA.

B

Bid/offer spread

With some funds there is a difference between the buying and selling prices of your units/shares. The price you buy the units at when you invest your money (the offer price) is normally higher than the price that you will get when you selling the units back (the bid price). This is because the fund manager will include an initial charge in his offer price. This pays for the setting up costs involved with your investment.

Blue chip companies

Many investment funds invest in these companies. They are usually large companies which are household names and which are considered to be stable. If they are based in the UK they will usually be in the FTSE 100 index.

Bonds

Bonds are loans to companies. In return for lending them your money you get paid a fixed rate of interest. The loan has a fixed term. This type of investment is also sometimes called a fixed interest security.

You can also lend your money to the Government. Then the loan is referred to as a gilt or gilt edged securities.

Capital

This is the amount of money you initially save or invest before any interest or growth is added.

Capital gains tax

This is the tax you pay on any increase in the value of some kinds of investments. There is an annual exemption limit which means that everyone can make a certain gain each year without paying the tax. This allowance changes each tax year.

Capital growth

The increase in the value of your investment, excluding any income after costs, charges and depreciation.

Child Trust Fund (CTF)

An Investment Product designed for children by the Government to encourage saving and investing (see Chapter 5).

Collective investment schemes

These are funds where the Investment Manager pools the money from a range of investors' together and invests it. Examples are unit trusts and ISAs.

Compounding

The way in which savings and investments grow over time because interest is added not only to the initial investment (your capital) but also to interest previously earned.

Corporate bonds

Fixed interest securities issued by companies. See Bonds.

Corporate bond funds

An Investment Manager's Fund invests in a range of different Bonds. Investments can then be made by Individual who buy units in this fund. This allows an individual to invest in a range of different Bonds, pooling their money with others rather than buying a smaller number of individual Bonds.

Coupon

This term refers to the fixed rate of interest payable by a Bond as a percentage of the value of the investment.

Credit ratings

When you buy a Corporate Bond you need to assess how likely it is that the company can meet its financial obligations in terms of paying you the rate of interest promised and returning your capital. Specialist credit agencies assess this to help you. The most secure companies will be given a AAA rating. The least secure will be rated as D (the least secure).

Credit risk

The rating given to a company when assessing how likely it is that the company can meet its financial obligations in terms of paying you the rate of interest promised and returning your capital.

Currency risk

Sometimes an Investment Manager will buy investments in other countries and this involves using the currency of the country concerned. There is a risk that the value of the investment will be affected if the exchange rate between the country concerned and UK Sterling changes.

Deposit account

This is another word for a Savings account available from a bank or building society.

Distributions

This is another way of referring to the income you gain in the form of interest or dividends when you invest in various Investment Products

Diversification

This means spreading your investment around so that you invest in different types of assets and/or different companies. By doing this you spread your risk. This means that you won't have all of your eggs in one basket.

Dividends
The income you get paid if the company you own a "share" in makes a profit.

Equities
Shares in a company. Also called stocks or stakes.

Equity exposure
This refers to the amount of your portfolio, or an Investment fund that is invested in equities, usually expressed as a percentage.

Exit charge
Sometimes also called a redemption charge. This is a charge made when you encash your investment. Not all investments involve a charge but you should check this before you make your investment.

Fact find

If you ask an IFA (independent financial adviser) for advice this is the way in which he or she finds out about your attitude to risk and savings goals by asking you some questions.

Financial Ombudsman Service (FOS)

If you are not pleased with the service/advice given to you by any firm authorised by the Financial Services Authority and they do not satisfy your complaint you can refer the matter to FOS who will investigate further on their behalf.

Financial Services Authority (FSA)

This is the body that has regulatory powers over financial advisers, investment and fund management companies, banks, building societies and insurers. All of these companies must follow and adhere to the rules set by the FSA.

Fixed interest securities

See Bonds

Friendly Society

Similar to a Life Assurance Company but with different tax rules.

FTSE 100 Index

The leading 100 UK Companies by market capitalization (the value of the shares they have issued) listed on the London Stock Exchange

FTSE 250 Index

The largest 250 companies by market capitalisation (the value of the shares they have issued) after those listed on the FTSE 100.

FTSE All Share Index

This refers to UK companies which are listed on the London Stock Exchange. Incorporates companies from the FTSE 100, FTSE 250 and FTSE Small Cap indices.

FTSE Small Cap Index

British index of the smallest companies by market capitalization (the value of the shares they have issued).

Fund manager

Sometimes called the Investment Manager. This person decides which direct investments should be put "inside the Box" when we invest in Investment Products.

Fund of funds

Fund of funds are designed to increase diversification. Instead of investing in direct investments the Fund Manager will invest in funds offered by other Managers. By doing this you spread the risk of relying on the expertise of just one Fund/Investment Manager.

Gilts

Bonds are issued by the UK Government in respect of loans made to them by individual investors. Also known as gilt edged securities. Along with bonds can be referred to as fixed interest securities.

Gross

Before tax.

Gross income

The amount of dividends and interest paid out to you before income tax has been deducted.

Half-yearly report

Also known as the "interim report". This lets you know what the fund you are investing in is trying to achieve and shows you how it has performed. The fund manager produces this during the financial year, before they prepare their Annual Report.

I

Income tax

This is the tax you pay to HM Revenue and Customs on any income you receive from your savings and investments. The amount you earn from employment and self employment is also taken into consideration when assessing the rate of tax you will pay.

Income units/shares

This type of unit/share will pay you any interest or dividends your investment has earned at regular intervals.

Index/indices

This is the word used to describe a group of shares or fixed interest securities on the stock market which are often similar in size or represent similar industries.

Index tracking funds

The objective of these funds will be to make your money grow by the same amount as the value of the companies listed on a stock market index, e.g. the FTSE 100. This is done by buying and selling shares in the same proportions as represented on the index. These are also sometimes called tracker, index or passive managed funds.

Independent Financial Adviser (IFA)

A Financial Adviser who will is authorised by the Financial Services Authority and will therefore be a qualified professional. They can survey all of the investments in the market place to advise which may be best for you.

Individual Savings Account (ISA)

An Investment Product where the "rules of the box" mean that it benefits from tax efficiency. ISAs replaced PEPs and TESSAs.

Inflation

A £1 coin will always be worth £1, but it's buying power will reduce as prices continually rise. This rise in prices is referred to as inflation.

Inflation risk

This is the risk that the interest rate added to your savings, bearing in mind tax may be payable, will be less than the rate at which inflation is rising. The spending power of your money would then be reduced.

Initial charge

The upfront fee that may be paid to an Investment or Fund manager when you make your investment. This is used to cover the initial expenses of investing and administering your money.

Investment/Insurance bonds

Not to be confused with Bonds (or Corporate Bonds). These are Investment Products. An Investment Bond is a lump sum investment, usually provided by a Life assurance company (sometimes referred to as an Insurance Company). Because
of the legal set up of their business the Investment Bond will also

guarantee that a sum of money will be paid out to you after a set term or upon death, even if this is only a nominal or negligible amount.

Interest

This is the money that a bank or building society will pay you in return for depositing your money with them. The amount will be expressed as a percentage of the amount that you have in your account. The income from Gilts and Bonds is also called interest.

Interest distributions

Income paid out by Investment Products when the direct investments held by the Fund Manager are cash, gilts and bonds.

Intermediary

When you buy a financial product you will very often do this via a third party (sometimes also called a Broker). This is instead of buying from the fund Management Company or Life Assurance Company directly. Normally, this will be because you have received advice from the third parties, though not always. Banks, building societies and independent financial advisers are the most likely third parties that you will use.

Investment funds

A Fund Manager will buy lots of different direct investments and place them inside their Fund (or Box). We can then buy units in these funds.

Investment trusts

Similar to unit trusts and OEICs. They are Investment Products which offer the chance to pool your investment. See Chapter 5.

K

Key features document

Before you reach a decision to make an investment you will be given a document which summarises all the key things you need to know about the investment including the risk and the charges that are involved. This allows you to make an informed decision.

L

Life Insurance Products

Life Insurance Companies (also known as Insurance Companies) offer investments. Because of the legal set up of their business all of the Investment Products they offer will also guarantee that a sum of money will be paid out to you after a set term or upon death, even if this is only a nominal or negligible amount.

M

Manager
See Fund manager.

Manager's report
Annual report and Half-yearly report.

Market capitalisation
The value of a company assessed by multiplying the number of the shares it has issued by the current value of those shares.

Market risk
Any investment which involves an investment in the stock market (i.e. in shares) or in Bonds can fluctuate in value and the returns are not guaranteed. This means that there is a risk that you might not make a profit and that you may not get back the amount of money that you invested.

Money market funds
An Investment Manager can choose to create a Fund where he or she invests directly in cash. These are often referred to as "cash funds"; they offer higher returns than a building society account as the Investment Manager benefits from buying in bulk and so can access good interest rates. Depending on the Investment Product (the "Box") that holds the Fund there may also be tax breaks.

Multi-manager funds

Normally used for Unit Trusts, though not always. These Funds are designed to increase diversification. Instead of investing in direct investments the Fund Manager will invest in funds offered by other Managers. By doing this you spread the risk of relying on the expertise of just one Fund/Investment Manager.

Multi-tied adviser

A type of financial adviser who can only sell you products from a limited number of financial institutions, rather than an independent financial adviser who can choose from all products on the market.

N

National Savings and Investments (NS&I)

These are a range of products offered by the Government. They are another way in which you can lend your money to the Government (the other is via Gilts). You receive a guaranteed return. There are many different products available but those most applicable to children are Premium Bonds and Children's Bonds.

Net income

The money you earn from dividends and interest after any income tax that is due has been paid.

O

OEICs

Open-ended investment companies. These are very similar to unit trusts, but are constituted as companies rather than trusts. For all intents and purposes this distinction is largely irrelevant to the average investor.

P

Personal Equity Plans (PEPs)

Tax efficient savings and investment plans which were replaced by ISAs in April 1999. PEPs taken out before that date remain valid, and benefit for tax efficiency but you cannot invest further funds into them. See also Tax wrappers.

Portfolio

As soon as you hold more than one type of investment, including a Bank of Building Society Account you can refer to your investments as a "Portfolio".

Provider

A generic term used to refer to the many different organisations who offer Savings and Investments. This includes Banks and Building Societies, Investment companies and Life Assurance (or Insurance) companies.

R

Redemption charge
See Exit charge.

Redemption date
For Gilts and or Bonds, the redemption date is the date in the future, usually set at outset, when the loan that you have made will be repaid and you get your investment back.

Regulator
See Financial Services Authority.

Return
The amount of income, capital growth or both that is generated by your investment.

Risk profile
Most investments involve some form of risk. One way in which we select or deselect them is with reference to the risk involved in relation to the risk that we are prepared to take. This is referred to as our Risk

Profile or attitude to risk.

Risk rating

See Credit rating.

S

Sectors

Investment Funds can have a huge number of different objectives in terms of how they intend to make your money grow. The Funds are divided into categories, known as sectors, depending on what these objectives are. This makes it easier to compare the performance of one fund manager with another. Categories may be geographical (e.g. UK Equity, European Equity) or refer to a specific industry (e.g. Telecommunications, Mining)

Securities

The collective name for Shares and Bonds

Shares

The 'bit' of a company you get in return for your investment. Also known as Stocks, Stakes, or Equities

Stakeholder

Some investment products (e.g. ISAs, Child Trust Funds, and

Pensions) are issued following guidelines put into place by the Government. This ensures that the products are low cost. With CTFs and pensions, procedures are put into place so that risk is limited during the latter years of the investment.

Stocks
Shares (also known as equities or stakes)

Tax wrapper
The Rules of the Box for some Investment Products mean that there is an extra layer of wrapping which shelters your interest and growth from paying certain taxes. Such products include pensions, ISAs, PEPs and TESSAs and Child Trust Funds (CTFs).

Tax year
6th April one year till 5th April the following year.

TESSA
A type of savings account with special tax privileges. No longer available but replaced by the cash ISA.

Tied agent
A type of financial adviser who can only sell you products from the

company he or she represents rather than the whole of the market.

TOISA

An Individual Savings Account which accepts transfers from TESSAs without affecting the individual's annual ISA limit. See TESSA.

Tracker funds

See Index tracking funds.

U

Units

Investment funds are divided into 'units' of equal value. Instead of buying one or two direct investments, your investment buys very small segment (or units) of a very much larger number of investments.

Unit trust

This is an Investment Product where the Investment Manager invests in a range of different direct investments. These investments are collectively known as an Investment Fund. Instead of buying one or two of the direct investments in the fund in their entirety, your investment buys very small segments (or units) of all of the investments. In this way you pool your money with that of others. Because this allows you to buy a small share in a greater number of investments you diversify and spread your risk.

W

With profits

A with-profits fund is an Investment fund offered by a life (or insurance) company. With-profits funds pool together premiums paid by a number of investors, which the insurance company then invests in a very wide range of assets.

Y

Yield

The amount of income being generated by your savings or investment. Usually expressed as a percentage of the original amount that you invested.

"Dad, when do I stop being a wholly owned
subsidiary of you and Mum?"

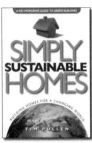

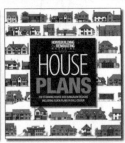
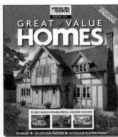
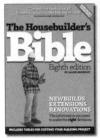

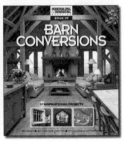